Read Me

University of Sydney Anthology 2011

SYDNEY UNIVERSITY PRESS

First published 2011 by Sydney University Press
in association with
Master of Publishing Program, the University of Sydney
School of Letters, Art and Media, the University of Sydney

Sydney University Press
Fisher Library F03
University of Sydney NSW 2006 AUSTRALIA
Email: sup.info@sydney.edu.au
Web: sydney.edu.au/sup

National Library of Australia Cataloguing-in-Publication entry

Title:	Read me: University of Sydney anthology 2011 / University of Sydney
ISBN:	978-1-920899-88-2 (pbk.)
Subjects:	Australian literature--21st century--Collections
Other Authors/Contributors:	University of Sydney
Dewey Number:	A820.8

Lines from 'Do Not Go Gentle into That Good Night' by Dylan Thomas, *Collected Poems*, 1934–1953, London: JM Dent, 1988.

Printed in Australia

Contents

Foreword

There may well be authors who write without the wish to be read, but I've yet to meet one. We write because we want someone, somewhere, to read me.

In bookshops and libraries lined up in neat rows according to author or genre or sales, the books we write wait, all expectant, each one with its own distinct voice saying — read me.

The title of this anthology is well chosen. It can be taken as an instruction to read the text that follows, or as a challenge to read beyond the writers' words and the stories they tell, to read the writer — read me.

For many writers this collection is their first opportunity to ask a broader audience — read me. To get this far is an achievement. It is also an act of courage because to write, is to risk. Anyone who has ever written something and shared it, with a class, or a writing group, will know the sense of dread involved in handing it over, perhaps even reading it aloud, offering it up to be considered, edited, judged.

All the writers in this collection have risked this process. They have submitted their work, one amongst many, for others to choose. They have opened themselves up to be edited and now they ask strangers — read me.

Despite knowing that this anthology was not collated with a particular theme in mind, as I read I began to sense that the struggle to establish, maintain or even survive relationships lay at the heart of many of the works.

The relationships encompass those that exist between family and friends, between lovers and enemies, or as is the case of Rob Ashton's 'BBQ Man' - narrated in a tone of self-deprecation but never self-pity — a struggle to establish the most basic relationship with the world.

A student anthology allows freedoms in form and expression; it provides space to experiment, to play. It grants latitude to write outside the boundaries of length, allowing the reader to appreciate brief but beautiful moments, such as the father and son's relationship in Connie Ye's 'Cinematic Ordeal', and the love of 'Darren, Boy Astronaut' for his mum in Patrick Hsiao's poem. The poetry, matched by beautiful images, is a highlight of the collection. I defy you to read Louise Carey White's 'Good Dirt' and not long to bury your feet in the real good dirt of home.

The title *Read Me*, I am told, is a nod to Alice's cake marked 'Eat Me', so it is appropriate that not only mad hatters, courtesy of Harriet McInerney, but other fantastical worlds find their way into this collection. There is Thomas Azzopardi's 'The Machine that Kept on Learning' and Ashley Kalagian Blunt's 'On the Wind' and then there is the world of Michela Ziady's 'Stone in Her Chest' which may seem fantastical, but is in fact all too painfully real.

When we write about what we care about, about what we think and feel, about what we believe, we perform an act that promises a connection to the consciousness of another human being. We offer a glimpse into the mind of another, a chance to feel as they feel.

But it is a risk.

There is the risk that the words will fall short, that the attempt to create something will fail and fail publicly. This is the risk. We may ask to be read but we cannot count on being received with approval, pleasure or even understanding. In the end all we can ask is — read me.

PM Newton

Harmonica Man

Isabel Robinson

Harp man he
puff on a cheap cigar
in the down-home stink
of a Dixie bar
curdled with sweat and moonshine
sour on the breath of the crowd.

In the wail of his harp hear
the beggar shake his lonely bowl,
the whistle of a vanishing diesel,
the bow-legged, big-eyed children
hanging round the shanties
on the edge of the falling sun.

Lighting strikes of high sharp sound
skewer the cracked heart
of the edgy whore,
she dance in the juke joint
with the packed earth floor and
the gutted piano.

Harmonica man he slide and bend those notes,
third hole deeper than a grave,
and when the tune is done
and the whisky drunk
and the bar closed,
it leave the taste of melancholy
on the tongue.

Ode to Cabbage

Laura Chan

White as winter,
Folded inside herself like origami,
The sleeping cabbage dreams easy
Of leaping out of the garden into
The hungry dark.

Leaf by leaf,
Unravelling string,
Story by story,
Princess and thief,
Nestled in her snug parabola,
She travels tundra;
Singing of sticking out squalls,
Of solitude,
And the corners of soft sunny beds.

She yearns
For white hills,
and black rivers buried
In the folds of the earth.
Silver snow sinks into grey waters,
And melts away with the wilting night.

Cabbage imagines herself
A star, ferried
Across the Milky Way:
From here the earth is a lantern —
Blue light moves from its centre
And through the cellophane sea.

Aboard the SS *Sillibabsss*

Thomas Azzopardi

The second the seventh ship had sunk
The sailors sang a song.
A song of simple, satirical verse
It hadn't been sung for long.

A story, a story, a story is told,
A story of sailors at sea.
The story is silly but serious at times
So I suggest you listen to me.

There once were sixty-seven sailors
Sicilians born and bred.
They set sail for Sydney on the sixth of the sixth
And their voyage goes as says.

The single and certain situation of sailors
Seems stranger than some would suggest.
As the story of the sixty-seven Sicilians
Succinctly surmises at best.

On the seventh day of the seventh week
Of the trip bound for Sydney's shores.
The sixty-seventh of the Sicilian sailors
Saw something, he wasn't quite sure.

Startled by the scene this shocked sailor saw
He scurried to his second mate's bed.
'Salvatore!' he screamed 'the sight I have seen!
Come see for yourself,' he said.

The second he said this Salvatore seemed certain
The sight about which he exclaimed.
'Seems simple to see that the startling scene
Is the Sambuca swimming in your brain!'

But since the circumstance stood steadfast for both,
The sailor got up to go see.
Though sceptical, cynical and set in his ways
He saw to his fellow man's plea.

'Though surely this sight has the same source as stumbling
And other seen signs of the drink.
I will see to this scene in case it is serious
And bids our fair vessel to sink.'

But the sight that he saw was as real as the sea
And immediately he sought for his sword.
But such was the speed of the creature in sight
That it soon enough slithered on board.

The creature then sang its siren song
Which sent the men mad as can be.
In a sad surrender to the soul shattering sound
The men hurled themselves to the sea.

But the sixty-seventh sailor stayed strong and sought
Revenge on the savage beast.
'My sixty-six brothers succumbed to your screeching
But I will confront you at least!'

Suddenly the song sharpened and the monster began thrashing
The sorely weather-worn ship.
Its temper grew vicious, it shook the starboard sternly
And the sixty-seventh knew this was it.

He stuttered 'we are but mere sailors of service,
For each soul we sincerely toil.'
Then the beast seized the hull
And screamed once and for all
'You shall never reach Sydney's soil!'

Sleepers in the Sand

Annabel Carr

Cinematic Ordeal

Connie Ye

He tried to stand close, but not too close. Just close enough to imagine that he could feel the warmth emanating from his father's body, and smell that familiar old man scent. He was facing his left shoulder at a forty-five degree angle, trying not to look at the letter he had gingerly proffered minutes before, nor at his father's face — bent over and inscrutable.

He looked down instead. His father's untucked shirt hung loosely around his waist. He didn't dare touch him, but had he reached out, he could have held on to his shirt. The way he might have clung to him as a child. Or he might never have done such a thing.

He tried to envision a positive end to the whole ordeal. Maybe a gruff nod and smile, a meaningful pat on the back. Or even better, a brief awkward hug full of the things left unsaid. How very lovely, how very cinematic that would be. Then they'd part and go on with the day, knowing that things could be different. But, distracting himself as he did, his mind persisted on wandering back to the words he had laboured over for the past two weeks. Just the introduction had kept him awake for a night. Should he call him Father? Dad? Old fella? Sir?

In the end he had opted for a casual 'Hey Dad', but the two short syllables felt kitsch and didn't seem to fit. He certainly regretted them now. It would set the tone for the whole thing all wrong. He had handwritten it on fine, thin paper, his writing shaky from the unaccustomed feeling of a pen in his hand. It was a page long. The sheer length was another thing to regret — brevity was the ultimate test of character in their household.

Hey Dad,

It might be a little bizaare that I'm writing this, but hear me out. It's been tough the past few weeks, and we know it's been the toughest for you. Grandpa was a wonderful man, I'm sorry I didn't get to know him better. I know I'm not in the right position to speak comfort, because he wasn't my dad. Nor can I imagine — this I know all too well because I'm not you. I can't know where to begin. Regardless, it must have been hard to not have been able to be with him and say a proper goodbye in the end.

When I was eight, Mum shot this video of us in the backyard at the old place. It was nothing special; it's you sitting on the bench fixing up the lawnmower, that stupid thing that always gave out when we pushed it onto the pebbles. You're sitting there doing your business, and I'm sitting next to you, tiny and completely attentive to your every move. To be honest I look a bit afraid of you, afraid to even move or say something that might distract you from your work, but the rest of my expression, about ninety per cent of my face, is pure adoration. Every now and then you ask me for a screwdriver, or some sandpaper, and quick as magic it's in your hands. There's something between father and son there in that video, something potent and beautiful.

Anyway Mum and I know you and Grandpa would have liked to have been closer. You know it already, but we're here for you, as always.

He hoped the letter made sense. He hoped he hadn't gotten himself confused with so many past tenses. He had avoided inserting any obvious sentiment on his part. He had hoped it would come naturally to his father as he read it. But most of all, he didn't want the moment to end. He had left the letter unsigned — like a romantic fool, he had been hoping that his father would simply keep reading and he could stand there, close and beside him.

His father's eyes roamed to the end, then back over the page, before the old man folded it up carefully and 'surprisingly' returned it to him.

Then, in an action that gave him unspeakable delight, his father's hand reached out and clasped his own for a split, lingering second.

'You spelt bizarre wrong, son.'

For once the crisp reminder of failure could not mask the inherent affection beneath. And that was enough, for now.

A Series of Small Cuts

Harriet Westcott

15 December 2006

I was a journalist for a brief time after I graduated from Imperial College London, and I reported the war, whilst wearing combat trousers, for a broadsheet. Based in Iraq, I learnt how to relay only half the story, and how not to panic in an emergency, both skills that are essential in my current job. Most people would not consider I had lived in a war zone, to look at me now. I know this. They see my hair, carefully styled and tied back from my face in a small knot at the back of my head. They see my face, made pretty with eye shadow, curved brows and sweeping lashes, my lips glossed with lipstick, smiling over whitened teeth. They see my uniform. The navy skirt carefully cut to just above the knee and which skims against my legs, revealing through a slash to one side the flesh-coloured nylon enshrouding my left thigh as I walk. The crisp white shirt that is sheer enough to suggest what might be underneath, with an opening at the neck that plunges in a downward arrow towards my chest. The company scarf wound tightly at my neck, decorated with a miniature motif that repeats over and over again across the shiny fabric: an aeroplane. I look neat, but enticing. I am appealing, but assured. I do not know you, but I am paid to look after you for a period, before sending you on your way.

I spotted you first on the way to Barcelona. Your enthusiasm stood out. Of all the other disinterested passengers, you were one of those who are unashamedly inquisitive. At that time, I was annoyed by your earnest approach to the safety demonstration. From behind you, I stared at the side of your head, willing it to slump with boredom instead of positioned alert to read the instructions on the screen played out on the seat in front of you. It did not. I felt derisive and tired, annoyed at having to watch a colleague politely answer your questions about something which seemed to you important. I omitted to properly check the seatbelts of the people occupying rows 39 to 50 on my way to the back of the plane, where I took my place for take-off.

You were a vegetarian, so although you were not in my section, I inadvertently found myself waking you for dinner as I pulled down your tray table and placed your meal before you. I did not know your name until then. Against my distaste, I was engaged by the way you looked as you stirred to consciousness. I felt my head craning forward towards yours in a brief moment of intimacy, to read your thoughts as you awoke. I did not think of you further on that flight. I left the stuffy cabin for the mild night air and ventured towards a cafe where I enjoyed a solitary coffee and a cognac, before wandering back to the hotel where I went to bed without showering or removing my makeup.

14 December 2007

I'd been doing North America for some time, when I found myself heading back to Barcelona. It can be like that. For some reason certain staff get stuck in a particular route, and just when the new one seems comfortable and familiar, they change it back to what it was before. There are fewer of us, now, on a flight. With economic rationalisation we work the same hours, but with the greater responsibility of more bodies to tend to. My rows started at the wing, and extended right to the back.

I remember on that flight I had two unaccompanied minors. We always seat them near the rear galley, ostensibly so we can keep an eye on them; in reality so they are away from the other passengers. You were speaking to one of them as you waited to use the toilet. I smiled as I slid past you, a genuine smile rather than the one I give to the other fliers, and inquired if I had seen you on this route before. You told me that you always travel with us, to Barcelona for a conference at this time of the year. Just for a few days. We chatted briefly. The aircraft was full and I did not stop smiling or walking the aisles for most of the flight.

It was a coincidence that you were staying at the same hotel. I had a weekend layover, which is rare nowadays, and I was keen to do some shopping and milling around. That time of the year is so beautiful in Barcelona, the sun bright and the sky blue, but still cool enough to wrap up in scarves and cosy sweaters. I spotted you in the morning at breakfast: me late, just as the buffet was being packed away, you full of croissant and raring to go. Somehow we exchanged numbers, and on my last night went for a drink. At a table too large for two, in a quiet bar, we talked. I asked about the marks on your arms and you told me that you had made them yourself with bits of broken glass. I didn't ask why. I looked at my own arms. I thought I knew what might drive someone to do that. We were silent. You wanted to go to back to the hotel, so we left, and that was that.

12 December 2008

I was willing you to be on the plane. On and off, whilst trying not to, I had been thinking about you for the whole year. I had been doing New York and Boston, but literally two days before they had switched me back from long haul to Europe. I was flying to Barcelona on a late flight again. I'd tried to read over the passenger list as we were setting up, but there was no time and, with over 300 people on board, there were too many names to scan. I was agitated.

You were not on that flight. I had felt foolish, imagining that I would see you, and I had deliberately pushed you to the back of my mind since then. It was with some great joy, then, that I found you seated in my section the following week.

I made a point of talking to you during the flight, after the meals were out of the way. You were at the window, so I had to lean over the other two passengers. It was hard to talk discretely from this position and above the burr of the engine, but all the same I asked if you would like to meet in Barcelona. You suggested that I come to your hotel that night, and the man seated next to you smirked as I told you to wait for me in arrivals, next to the newsstand which would by now be closed. I pretended not to hear his request for another gin and tonic as I retreated to prepare for landing.

There is something provocative about the blandness of a hotel bedroom. The furnishings in neutral colours, set out with just exactly what you need for a short stay, a bible in the drawer by the bedside in case of insomnia. Those cotton sheets, smelling slightly of washing powder, pulled so tightly against the mattress that to get into bed engenders a feeling of being strapped into it. It was in one of those rooms that we talked, and talked, and talked. I told you about the attacks, and how it was to see whole buildings crumble in seconds. And the wailing afterwards, which cut right through to the bone. I'd never written about that in an article. I sat in the armchair, next to the desk, hardly comfortable, squirming myself about in an ongoing attempt to attain a degree of relaxation. I was still in my uniform. You perched on the bed opposite.

There came a point after midnight when I was just too exhausted to talk anymore, even though I wanted our conversation to reach to the moon and back. I could never tire of staring at your face and watching your eyes as they conveyed the excitement in your voice, but age is a killjoy and there came a point in those timeless hours when I had to admit the end. You acknowledged that you were also tired. You sat on the bed, head bowed, for a minute, rummaging through your papers, perhaps checking something for the next day. I walked out without saying goodbye.

13 December 2009

Sitting on the crew shuttle I am facing backwards en route to the airport. I smile indulgently to myself, thinking of the lipstick marks still on my chest, stomach, and around my right breast. You had said you wanted to eat my heart. Finally, after all this time. Last night you had been cheeky, going through my carry-on tote and pulling out the standard items that we are issued. You grimaced at the lipstick, protesting that it was horrendous in colour, and surely not one I had chosen. I explained that the company issues us with not only a uniform, but also makeup. We have to wear one of two shades of lipstick. The other shade is better suited to those of a lighter complexion. You guffawed and pretended to vomit in the small bin beside the bed. I laughed. I told you that our hair had to be tied in one of three styles: a bun at the base of the head, a low ponytail, or a French pleat. Hair spray must be used, to combat stray strands mid-shift. I explained that the only jewellery we are allowed to wear is a watch (either a metal or a leather strap, nothing coloured), and one ring on each hand, although for the purposes of those who are married, an engagement and wedding ring are permitted and counted as one. I finished by explaining that our grooming standards did not permit perfume, as some scents may offend passengers, but that deodorant was expected at all times.

You said that you wanted to get closer and see how I smelled. You said that you were a mystery customer tasked with checking staff body odour. You opened my lipstick, still in your hand, and smeared your lips with it, garish and thick. And then you unbuttoned my shirt.

You left early in the morning for the first flight back, and when I awoke, you had already packed and had a taxi waiting. I felt disorientated. I saw you had left your comb in the bathroom, and I wasted valuable time retrieving it for you. Don't leave without taking this I said, somewhat pointlessly. With a quick hug, you were out of the door. There is something on the table, were your last words to me as you dragged your suitcase into another world.

On the bus I look down at my hands, where I hold the cuttings you had clipped from the newspaper and left for me. They are annotated with your biro, in amusement at what the journalists had so clearly left out. It made me smile, that you had understood this.

As I arrive with the crew we are told that there will be delays. The airport is log jammed and it is unlikely we will fly tonight, so we are told to go to the staff lounge and wait, and not go through to customs as usual. Probably strikes. This sort of thing happens more often than it should, and whilst staying in a hotel for a planned layover is a delight, being forced to return because of a problem is a bind. Being on call for the next available flight means being trapped in the hotel indefinitely, waiting.

Sitting with a vending machine coffee in the lounge, I hear a steward from a rival rasping in a fake whisper to the stewardess next to him that it is such a shock that a plane has gone down. I start to listen. The plane had reported faults before take-off, but it is ultra busy at this time of the year, and cancellation costs the airline millions, so they had decided to run with it, thinking it would be okay. It usually is. But the plane had got into trouble during take-off, one of the engines had caught alight and the ailerons had failed on both sides, so the pilot had to emergency land. Because the runway is quite short, and there is no vacant space around the airport the plane had simply nosedived into the tarmac. 'Terrible,' he said. Right before the holidays with all those people going home to see their families. Children too. Gone. He tutted.

'Which flight was it?' I asked him.

He turned around to me, seemingly surprised that I was next to him. Looking at my uniform condescendingly for a second, before altering the impression of his face to one of sympathy, he answered: 'One of yours. London. Seven Oh Two. Earliest one out.'

And then I am called to gate.

On my break in the tiny rest room I pull your newspaper cuttings from my uniform pocket. I roll them into a ball, and stuff all four of them into my mouth. I stand before the sink, and chew the dry paper, retching slightly in my efforts to work up enough saliva to swallow them down. I can taste the greasy print. Next I clean my teeth so long and so hard that my gums start to bleed with the sheer force of the brush, and when I spit into the metal basin the foam is pink with my blood. Words flash across my mind, and seem to reflect back at me in the mirror. I take a shallow breath and smooth my hair. I re-tuck my shirt into the top of my skirt. I reach into my bag for my lipstick. I take it out. I pause. And then I throw it down the toilet. The flush makes a sizzling sound as it pulls my lipstick away, like the noise of bacon being thrown into a pan of hot oil. I slide open the little door, and walk out into the cabin, my eyes hard, smiling at the passengers with my lips bare.

the first emperor

Jacqueline Buswell

though I sought immortality this life ended at fifty
I bequeath to you my terracotta warriors
the entombed craftsmen are mocking me
two thousand years the clay stands — my story lives

I bequeath to you my terracotta warriors
I was a child king — no I was never a child
two thousand years the clay stands — my story lives
I trusted myself and my horses, none other

I was a child king — no I was never a child
I rode my chariots from palace to palace
I trusted myself and my horses, none other
I built a secret mud army to protect my spirit

I rode my chariots from palace to palace
giving names to mountains and prairies
I built a secret mud army to protect my spirit
and buried the craftsmen to conceal my treasure

I gave names to mountains and prairies
few then admired the folds of my warriors' dress
I buried the craftsmen to conceal my treasure
I sought elixirs to grant me eternal youth

few then admired the folds of my warriors' dress
the detail of face, headgear, limestone armour
I sought elixirs to grant me eternal youth
first emperor you call me but do you know my name?

exquisite detail of face, headgear, limestone armour
the entombed craftsmen are haunting me
first emperor you call me but do you know my name?
though I sought immortality this life ended at fifty

Only Letters

Alison Gibson

Benny was sitting on the floor in the lounge room, a scrabble board in front of her and all the tiles spread, face up, around her. She was picking out words and arranging them. She liked letters. Even though every adult she knew could read and write, letters still seemed like some sort of secret code. She loved the ways they could fit together, changing and shifting patterns on the board depending on which letters she chose to line up. Each time she hit on a particularly interesting combination her brain gave a sort of soundless pop, as though looking at a word in a completely new way caused a mini flare to go off.

A news theme jangled from the radio in the kitchen. It must be six o'clock, nearly dinner time. The twins were at the kitchen table with a pile of scrap paper and fat, waxy crayons. They both loved drawing, though neither of them were any better at it than she had been at five years old.

Her dad would be home soon. His bus always arrived at the bus stop at the top of the street just after the six o'clock news theme. Sometimes she would lean over the back of the couch, looking out the window to see his long silhouette, cast with the strong street light from outside the house next door, coming home. But tonight she wanted to use the 'z' tile for something other than 'zoo', and it was taking a lot of concentration. She tried a few combinations, but always seemed to need an extra 'z', for 'buzz', or 'snazzy', or 'jazz', and anyway, she wasn't sure they were real words. Just as her mother called out that dinner was ready she hit upon 'aztec'. They had been looking at the Aztecs in class, and she thought that it was probably meant to start with a capital letter, but decided not to worry about it. It was a fabulous word to have found, and she left the board set up in the hope that one of her parents would notice it.

Her dad was running late, apparently, so they were eating without him. Dinner was chicken stir-fry, with a thick, honey-flavoured sauce.

It was the twins' favourite, and they made loud slurping noises as they ate. Benny liked it too, but it was very sweet, and she tried to shake some of the sauce off a large clump of noodles. Sauce splattered over the tablecloth and her mum groaned, but not in a very angry way. 'Careful, Ben, or the twins will start licking the table.' Benny and the twins all started giggling at the thought, and Henry, the more rebellious twin, bent over as if he was going to lick the table, a mischievous look on his face. Petie covered his mouth with his hands in delight, but with a don't-you-dare sort of noise from his mum, Henry sat back in his chair. The radio had been turned down low, but Benny could still hear when the seven o'clock news theme started. Just as it was ending they heard a key in the door, and a loud 'hello' from her dad. Seven was very late for him to get home.

'In the kitchen,' Mum called back. Her dad seemed to fill the doorframe. He had on a heavy winter coat, which looked odd in the warm kitchen, but he didn't take it off. 'Susie, can I talk to you for a second?'

'Can it wait 'til the kids have had their bath?' Her mum barely glanced at him; she was too busy wiping sauce off Petie's face. Her dad looked strange. His face was very long. She had always thought this was a strange description of someone, as though at times someone's face could just grow longer. But tonight, her dad wasn't smiling, and was so far from smiling that it really did look as though his face had grown longer, and the corners of his mouth were almost drooping off the edge of his chin. His eyes were dark, or maybe that was just because his skin looked so pale.

'Come have some dinner,' her mum added, since he was still standing in the doorway. His shoulders dropped in a sigh but he didn't argue.

Benny poked a long snow pea with her fork and held it up to her mouth. Her dad kissed her forehead as she forced the entire snow pea into her mouth. It was too long, and it took a concerted effort to chew it without coughing. It had put sauce on either side of her mouth and she felt it start to dribble, but neither of her parents was looking at her. Her mum was starting to haul the twins off for their bath, and her dad was staring at his plate of stir-fry as though he was unsure what to do with it.

Bath noises drifted down the hallway. The twins were only just small enough to share a bath, and it could take some negotiation to get them both in and clean. Benny picked up a piece of broccoli with her fork and watched the sauce ooze out. 'Ooze' was another word with 'z', she would have to remember that for next time. Her dad breathed in noisily, as though his lungs didn't quite feel like breathing properly. 'Find any good words today, love?' He asked Benny. She grinned through a carrot.

'Aztec!' He nodded but his eyes were not focused on her.

'That's good. Good. Keep it up.'

Benny was a slow eater, and by the time she had finished the twins were out of the bath and in their pyjamas. Her mum went to read them a story, and shouted out for Benny to jump in the shower. She slid off her stool, her empty plate covered in globules of congealing sauce. Her dad had eaten one snow pea before replacing his fork exactly as it had been. Benny wondered if her mum would notice that the fork had been used, or if it would be put back in the drawer with faint traces of snow pea and honey sauce on it.

Benny had a super hot shower, turning the hot water up as high as she could without having to jump out of the way. Her skin turned pink and tingly, but still sent shivers down her spine. When she got out, she scrubbed herself down as quickly as she could with her towel. It was her towel because it was small but pretty, and the twins didn't care about pretty things. They had the plain yellow towels, but she got to use this green one with flowers in the corners. It was probably one of the prettiest things she owned. She wrapped the towel around her body and opened the bathroom door. She heard voices, getting louder and louder, coming from her parents' bedroom. They didn't usually go in there this early at night. She walked slowly down the hallway towards the door. The door was half closed — she had never seen it fully closed — and she could hear her dad talking insistently over the top of a strange noise. She paused at the door, looking in at her parents she realised that the strange noise was her mum crying. She had never heard it before. Her mum was sitting on the bed, her hands scrunching balls of doona on either side of her legs. Her mouth was wide open and she was sobbing. In movies whenever women cried they always covered their mouth with one hand and had a few tears running down each cheek. They never had a bright red face, or a mouth open and showing strings of saliva. And they definitely didn't make noises like that. Benny took a step back, afraid to go in. She leant against the wall, the plaster cold against her bare arms, which were still tingling from the heat of her shower.

Her dad was pacing back and forth in front of her mum, his hands running through his hair, and then tugging at his clothes. Benny felt a sour taste at the back of her throat which didn't go away when she swallowed. Her hair started dripping water down her back and a faint draught made her shiver. Her dad stopped talking. She stepped forward and pushed the door open a bit. Her stomach clenched tight at the sight of her mum. Her dad turned quickly, but her mum didn't seem to notice her. Her mum just turned and lay down on the bed, her legs still hanging over the edge. It looked strange and twisted, and she lay sobbing loudly into the doona cover. Benny couldn't stop looking at her, and the sour taste had taken over her whole mouth.

'Oh Benny, oh love, how was your bath?' She knew that her dad was forcing normality into his voice, but it grated strangely against his throat. She wanted to ask what was wrong with her mum, but her dad bent down and put an arm around her and swept her quickly out of the room. She tried to look over her shoulder to see if her mum was moving, but her dad's body was in the way. He pulled the towel closer around her. 'You'll catch a cold, you duffer. Where are your pyjamas?' He pulled her back down the hallway to her room. Once in there, he helped her put on her winter pyjamas, and then towel dried her hair. Her pyjamas were light blue with paw prints on them, and the material was soft against her skin. She twisted her arms in their sleeves to feel the softness. 'What's wrong with mum?' she asked. Her voice felt shrunken in her throat.

'Nothing love, she's just a bit upset.'

'Why?' He sighed and looked distracted. He rubbed his eyes, and the corners of his mouth dropped further down. He sighed again. How could he keep sighing when he didn't seem to be breathing in?

'Bernadette, I need you to go to bed, and go to sleep. Tomorrow we'll talk. But for tonight, I need you to just go to sleep.' Maybe he was mad at her for going into their bedroom, or for seeing her mum like that. She wanted to fling her wet towel at him and start crying herself. She felt squirmy from the discomfort of everything being slightly out of place. Her dad had already stood up though. He had obviously decided that she was going to bed. She dropped the towel and got into bed. The sheets were cold and she wriggled her toes furiously.

'Thank you,' he said, and kissed her on her forehead. On his way out of the room he picked up her pretty green towel from the floor.

***

Benny woke in the morning to noises of activity coming from the kitchen. She panicked, thinking that she had missed her mum's call to wake up. She pushed the heavy doona off her feet and shivered when her feet touched the wooden floor. She wrapped her dressing gown around her and shuffled out the door, trying not to trip over the long train. It was her cousin Margie's old dressing gown, and was far too long for her. It wasn't until she was in the kitchen that she realised the voices she had heard were those of her grandparents. With a squeak of delight she ran forward and gave each grandparent a hug. The twins were at the kitchen table, their breakfast spread around them in a large mess: cornflakes, milk, orange juice, breadcrumbs and a big dollop of jam. Her grandpa was trying to get Petie to eat his last square of toast. Her grandma was trying to clean up the table. They were both talking cheerfully. 'Where are Mum and Dad?' Benny asked while eating a spoonful of cornflakes.

'They just popped over to the doctor, Benny, they'll be back soon.'

'The doctor? What's wrong?' The feeling of the night before squeezed its way back into her stomach and her cornflakes became sour in her mouth.

'Oh, it's probably nothing dear. Your mum just asked us to come keep an eye on you bunch while she went with your dad. They'll be back soon and they can tell us all about it. But it means that you don't have to go to school today, isn't that exciting?' Her grandma had a lightness in her voice which didn't sound real, and she didn't make eye contact with Benny. Her grandparents didn't seem to know anything either, but it was good that they were there. If they were there they would talk about what was wrong, and then they could fix it. By the end of the day it would all be normal again. The thought didn't change the feeling in her stomach though. She had to force down more cornflakes so that she didn't attract the attention of grandpa and his spoon, which was famous for making delicate eaters eat.

Her grandma was making sandwiches for lunch by the time her parents got home. Benny and her grandpa were sitting at the table with the scrabble board, trying to find new words. She had just added 'ooze' running down from the 'o' in 'flower' when she heard the key in the door. She jumped up and went running. Petie came tearing down the hallway at the same time. 'I got "ooze"', she said proudly as her parents opened the door. Her mum just looked at her, confused, and didn't say anything. Her eyes were red and watery.

'That's great, honey,' her dad said, but he didn't sound like he thought it was great. Her grandparents appeared and looked expectant. Her mum pushed passed them though, and disappeared down the hallway and into the bedroom, with her grandma following closely behind. Her dad pulled her arm gently, and led her and her grandpa back into the kitchen. He sat, looking at 'ooze' and 'flower' on the scrabble board. The twins were running around, excited by all the people in the room.

'What is it Tom? Just say it,' her grandpa said. His voice was gruff. Benny looked back and forth between her dad and her grandpa, and hoped that no one would say anything. Their expressions were so sad that whatever they said would be sad too, and she didn't want anything to be sad. She wanted them to just make funny words with the scrabble pieces. Words like 'oink', and 'splat', which sounded like words from a cartoon and always made her giggle.

'It's HIV.' Her dad's voice was very quiet.

HIV wasn't a word, it was just letters. Benny sounded it out. H-i-v. It didn't sound that bad. It was so short. Her grandpa's face was extending slowly, getting longer and longer, his eyes and mouth drooping with it. Her mouth filled with sourness again.

'How?' There was a hard edge to the word, like her grandpa had cut it out of his lungs with a blunt knife. Her dad coughed, and stared at his hands.

'How?' her grandpa repeated. Her dad seemed to have stopped breathing.

'His name was Greg.' Her grandpa became so still it was like he was made of stone. Benny thought of the ice queen in Narnia and could almost see her draping long white cloth everywhere, standing behind the stone statue of her grandpa. A stone statue which still seemed to be radiating some kind of energy. Benny wanted to move away from him.

'What's Susie going to do?' His voice sounded like stone too, ragged and harsh as though it didn't come from flesh at all.

'She's staying. I told her everything last night. She was tested today but we won't know for a few weeks. She's staying.' Her dad shifted slightly in his seat, and faced out the window. His face was grey. Her grandpa stood up, and left the table. He went and stood at the kitchen sink, but didn't touch any of the dishes. From the bedroom they could hear sobbing and an angry voice. None of them spoke. The sobbing changed into yelling, but Benny couldn't hear the words. Her mum and her grandma were yelling at each other, she'd never heard that before. She looked out the window to what her dad was watching. There were two magpies sitting on the telephone wire, and a third one flying in and out, trying to play with them. The one on the left gave a sudden lunging peck and the flying one squawked and flew away.

The twins were wrestling on the floor, and had rolled halfway under her chair. She started yelling at them to stop. It felt good to yell, it made the silence go away for a while. After a minute or so her dad put his hand on her arm to make her stop. She felt tears on her face.

The yelling from down the hallway became louder suddenly as the bedroom door opened. Her grandma's voice reached them clearly for the first time. 'You don't owe him.' Benny could hear the spit in the words. Her grandma walked into the kitchen and grabbed her handbag from under the telephone table. 'C'mon George.' Her grandpa shuffled towards the door, looking much more like an old man than he had at breakfast that morning. Benny sat at the table, waiting for her dad to say something, or to remember that there were half-made sandwiches sitting on the counter waiting to be finished, but he didn't move. Her mum appeared in the kitchen, her face dark red, and sat at the table. Her dad reached over to hold her hand, but she pulled away.

'Benny, I need you to go play with the twins.' Her mum's voice was flat and hard. Benny didn't want to go. She didn't want to play with the twins, who had ceased rolling under the table and were now trying to get her dad's attention by pulling his socks up and down. Her mum didn't look at her though; she was staring at her husband, her hands tucked under the table. Benny called to the twins and left the kitchen. She wanted to stay and talk about 'hiv' and what was going on, but instead she pulled out a stack of scrap paper and crayons and sat on the floor with the twins, drawing coloured, waxy figures.

An Unwelcome Friend

Sarah Bendall

The room was cold and smelt like stale urine. She looked into the cracked mirror under pale iridescent lights and studied her face. The green eyes that sat behind heavy brows stared back at her. Her freckled skin glowed under the lights next to her small, rose-coloured lips. Running her fingers through the red hair that sat atop her head she poked, prodded, teased and preened until it was just right. Everything had to be just right. She had waited so long for this. She wasn't going to let a fly-away strand ruin her night; nor the return of an unwelcome friend.

'Or will you?'

She whirled around but there was nothing behind her. The bathroom of the old cinema was empty, only the sounds of a broken faucet and the constant flow of water through the septic system could be heard. She was beginning to think that maybe even after all this time she really was crazy. She closed her eyes. Maybe her afternoon had all been a hallucination?

***

Her day at university had been, quite frankly she thought, shit. Bad marks for a paper, another one due soon, a fight with her closest friend, indifference from another, headache, cold coffee, and missed appointments had all ruined her day. To round it all off heavy rain had spilt from the grey skies, each drop hitting her face harder than the last, until after only a matter of minutes she had been soaked through. If this hadn't been enough, afterwards she was forced to endure overcrowded and stuffy lessons with wet socks, wet clothes and lousy heating. As she left her last class a familiar feeling swept over her. The excited, nervous and trembling sensation that she got every time she thought of him; the feeling that travelled from the pit of her stomach through her chest and limbs making her palms sweat. She looked at her watch. Only four hours to go.

'Hi Hun, how was your day?' her mother inquired from the lounge as she closed the front door behind her and walked through the dark hallway to her room. 'It was fine, Mum,' she lied as she unwrapped a grey scarf from her neck and hung it on a hook behind her door before closing it, shutting out the rest of the world. She placed her bag of books next to the old oak desk in the corner of the white-walled room. She heard a creak from the old wooden boards that covered the bedroom floor and turned around in alarm.

A soft scream left her lips, muffled only by the hand she placed over her mouth. It was a dark, ashen face, with dry scales like that of a fish stuck on land too long, it stunk of rotting flesh. Its eyes were yellow with black, oval shaped pupils, whose depths seemed endless if one stared long enough.

'Are you okay in there?' her mother yelled from down the hallway. Her heart thudded loudly within her chest. 'Just a spider,' she said, slowly exhaling what she could of the heavy breath that had caught in her lungs.

In front of her stood something she thought she had banished; an old friend who she'd sworn would not disturb her anymore.

'Did you miss me?' The thing said as it turned its head to the side, its snake-like tongue darting out behind sharp teeth and baiting words.

She closed her eyes and shook her head. No, it wasn't there, she was just hallucinating; she mustn't have eaten enough.

'Well?' said the creature that stood in front of her.

'Wha — , what? I … I don't understand. How did you get back? Why are you here?' The creature paced back and forth between the desk and her bed.

'Not even a hello? That's quite rude you know. But as for the question of why and how, we have far too much history, you and I, for that to warrant an answer. Hmm … ' The creature finally settled for sitting on the flower-covered spread of her bed, crossing its legs and rearranging the slightly dusty, black cloak that it wore before continuing, 'the reason I'm here — I think we both know the answer to that question.'

She ran her fingers through her hair in frustration and looked at the clock above her door. Three hours until she was supposed to be at the cinemas.

'But with all the time that's passed, and with what happened before. I thought I'd got rid of you.'

The creature grinned, flashing those jagged teeth. 'We are not something you can just get rid of, my dear. We are far more resilient than that, quite like a virus. We may lay dormant for periods of time. But disappear entirely? Rarely does that ever happen.'

She wasn't crazy. She wasn't crazy. Oh God please let her not be crazy, she thought. She pinched herself just to make sure.

'I can assure you this is all quite real,' the creature said as it fingered the detailed carvings of a snow globe, which sat on her bedside table. It depicted a family playing. The thing grabbed it with long skinny fingers and shook it viciously.

'What do you want from me then?'

'What do I want? You, my dear, seem to have forgotten a little bargain that we made years ago. Do you remember it? I see you do. You know you must really learn not to give away everything with your eyes; they're windows to the soul, as they say.' It stared at her. Those black slits were like an abyss.

'Your eyes don't. You have no soul.'

The creature clapped its hands together. 'Well done! See, we are learning more and more about each other as time goes by … Like,' it placed a finger to its lips as its hand rested on the tuff of hair on its chin, 'I know that you are going on a little date tonight with that boy from your class. What is his name? Chris?'

'Yes?' She became slightly unnerved, 'and what about it?'

'Well, as much as I'd like to see you happy, that's just not in my line of business, now is it?'

'But he's got nothing to do with anything.' She knew deep down though that he did, he made her happy and it had a problem with that.

'Let me spell it out for you then,' the creature continued, talking to her as if she were a small child, 'I'm the bad guy and what do supernatural bad guys usually want?' It looked at her, expecting an answer. She didn't give one.

'To put it simply, I want your soul — your life force, your happiness, everything you ever were and will be. I want that, and I want to control it and twist it into my own darkness.'

'You really enjoy this, don't you?'

'Well,' it said smiling wickedly, 'they don't call me a Demon for nothing, Darling.'

She was beginning to feel more in control now that the shock had started to wear off. Who was it, this thing, to think that it could just reappear and ruin her life all over again?

'I won't let you get to me.'

'I did once before.'

'But that was then and there's no way that I'm going to give you what you want now. So just get the fuck out of here and leave me alone!'

Her chest heaved and she felt like she had just told her high school bullies to shove it. The adrenaline pumped through her veins and she felt powerful and confident. The Demon looked at her, its nostrils flared, and suddenly it seemed larger than before, and even more menacing.

'I won't leave you this time. You'll see.'

She turned to her desk, ready to grab something to throw at it. But when she turned back there was her bed, wardrobe, bookshelf, floor rug and heater but no Demon, it was gone. Surely it had just been the product of her tired mind?

***

The iridescent lighting hurt her eyes as she opened them. She was still in the stinking cinema bathrooms. Shaking her head, she looked down at the watch that she wore on her slender wrist. The needle slowly ticked in time with her heartbeat. Looking back into the mirror she could see her cheeks starting to turn a shade of red. Ten more minutes. Ten more minutes and she would be meeting Chris.

Her heart started to pound within her chest, its frantic beats left the ticking hand of her watch out of sync. She quickly rearranged the navy dress that she wore, adjusted the brown belt around her waist, took one more glance in the mirror and turned to the door that led into the cinema foyer.

He had told her to wait outside, near the main entrance. He would be there at exactly 8pm. As she walked outside she passed smiling couples holding hands, young teenagers with giant buckets of popcorn that would soon end up on the theatre floor or in somebody's hair. Mothers stood at the candy bar with crying children, ushers took people's tickets, old men with walking canes, young girls with their older sisters, brothers, fathers, cousins and grandmothers. She walked alone through the crowds of people though, unnoticed and undisturbed, until she reached the cinema entrance.

Standing outside the cold wind blew and she felt goose bumps rise on her arms. She did not know if it was the wind or the excitement that caused her body to react in such a way. Looking back at her watch she noted, five minutes. Only five minutes to go.

'You know you really shouldn't wear that dress, it does nothing for your colouring, Darling.'

There it was again, its tall figure reflected in the glass windows as it stood next to her at the cinema entrance. The fifties-era neon lights cast a blue shadow over its disgusting face. She looked around but nobody else seemed to notice the black figure as they made their way through the revolving doors and into the warmth.

'You know they can't see me. I'm your Demon, not theirs, although I bet some of this lot have a few of their own.' It sniffed members of the crowd, scanning them with its freakish eyes as they shuffled past.

'Oh God, maybe I am crazy,' she said, running her fingers through her hair. She looked at her watch. It wasn't long now. She needed it to go away, if only for a little while.

In desperation and with wide eyes, she begged: 'Go away, please. The last thing I need right now is you here.'

'Sorry, but you're the one that summoned me ... what with that little display in the bathrooms.' She looked at her watch. 8pm, it was time. But he wasn't here; maybe he was just running late. She would stand there and wait a bit longer until he came. Meanwhile she tried to ignore the Demon and its taunts.

'He's not going to come, deep down you know that right?'

'Shut up, he will come, I know he will.'

But he didn't.

It was now 8:15pm; the wind was starting to blow harder, sending rust coloured leaves dancing down the footpath.

'He's still not here.' It stood behind her, leaning against a glowing poster box. 'I don't think he's coming. Admit it, you were wrong ... as usual.'

She placed her hands over the red tips of her cold ears, blocking out its words. 'This isn't happening, don't listen ... you're pretty, you're fun, you're interesting — '

'You're boring,' it cut in.

'No I'm not and he is coming, I like him and he likes me, I know he does, he wouldn't have asked me out otherwise.'

'Really? You honestly believe that? Darling, look at yourself and think of him, he could have any girl he wanted but he chose you?'

'He wants me — '

'Darling, nobody wants you.'

Its words hit her like a slap in the face. She couldn't take it anymore. She needed to be somewhere other than here. Tears welled behind her tired eyes, but they didn't fall. They hadn't for months, not since it had visited her last time.

Turning, she ran, down the broken cement footpath, past the cinema entrance and takeaway shop, until she reached a red pedestrian sign. The city moved around her, the cars, the buses, the crowds and crowds of people, lights, beeps, shouts, cries, tears, laughter — but she stood still. She was stuck, unable to move forward with the crowds, overlooked and unappreciated.

'You might as well stand in the middle of that road over there and scream — nobody will care'.

The weight of realisation bore down upon her shoulders. She was alone.

***

Loud sounds and flashing images illuminated the dark hall as she snuck back into the house quietly, so not to disturb her mother, who sat in lounge room watching television. She closed the damp ridden door of the moss-green bathroom, turned taps and let the warm water flow while she sat on the side of the bathtub and studied herself in the mirror that rested on the vanity opposite. Black lines of mascara, as well as the other parts of her daily mask, ran down her face. The reflection seemed to mock her. Her hair was wild and messy, her eyes were swollen and red. The belle after the ball. This is what Cinderella would have looked like if she had been stood up and humiliated by her Prince Charming, she thought grimly.

The clock above the mirror ticked. Shiny steel glistened below the bathroom cabinet.

'Look at it.' The Demon now sat next to her on the edge of the bathtub; she could smell its rancid breath as she looked at the old-fashioned shaving blade.

She wouldn't do it. She wouldn't go back to that. But the darkness — her Demon — told her otherwise. 'You know you want to.'

'No, I won't do it, never again. I made a promise,' she said as her hands twisted and pulled against each other in her lap.

'But you know how much better you will feel afterwards,' she felt its breath on her ear now, 'you know what it can do.'

Her fingertips became clammy, and her body ached for what the cool steel blade would bring, her own orgasm — a release.

'Here, let me help you,' it said, appearing a second later before her, the razor in its hand, offering it to her.

'No, I won't do it.'

'Really? You don't seem so sure,' it grabbed her hand and placed the handle inside. She felt the familiar weight of cold steel as it forced the blade down to the white skin of her forearm.

She struggled against it, attempting to free her hand from its grasp. 'Let me go,' she screamed as she kicked and struggled against it. She nearly thought she had won, nearly beaten the frightening and powerful force that made her hold the blade so close to her flesh. But it was too strong, too powerful for her to resist, she didn't have the strength or the will to fight it. Finally she gave up and let the Demon have its way.

'There you go, that's a girl.'

She looked up at her somewhat pathetic reflection in the mirror as her shaking fingers, cradled in the cold, claw-like hand, lowered to her arm. Ignoring her reflection, she looked back down and watched the thin, cold blade slide over her pale skin. Feeling the blood flow from the wound, it was like releasing a poison. No, it was more than that, as if the bright red substance that escaped her veins released what crying couldn't. All those built up emotions, all those things she wanted to say and do, but couldn't, all the self-doubt, the hate that was inside. As she sat there with the cloaked figure watching over her, it was like all those things were slowly being released through the liquid that sustained what made her endure it all — life.

At that moment, in her bedroom, on her floral covered duvet, in the fake suede clutch that lay atop it, her phone flashed 8:40pm and the caller ID listed the name 'Chris'. If she had still been outside that cinema on that cold autumn night, with the traffic, the crowds, the popcorn and the laughter, she might have seen a boy with flowers, anxiously trying to contact her. Wondering why she hadn't picked up her phone all night. But she wasn't. It was too late.

Instead she had run, letting her Demon get the better of her. And now she sat, slumped up against the cold, green tiles of the bath tub, like a user with her release, her own fucking brand of heroin. The tides of emotions had washed away, leaving emptiness. She was numb, and she knew like a crack addict itching for another hit that she wouldn't be able to resist anymore.

Blood ran from the cut and onto the floor tiles.

The Demon crouched next to her, its black cloak grazing her thigh. A long, twisted finger jutted out from a black sleeve and traced over the wound. It pulled back, red with blood, putting it to a barbed tongue.

'You'll be a good girl won't you now, Darling?' It said touching her limp hair, her delicate eyelids, her button nose and pale cheeks. Finally it kissed her rosy lips with its rough mouth and whispered, 'I'll be seeing you again soon. You're mine now.' Then it was gone.

***

At another plain house, in another quiet suburban street, a young man stood in his clean white bathroom at exactly 9pm brushing his teeth. The bristles moved back and forth, in and out, removing the stains of daily life. When finished he rinsed, gargled and placed his toothbrush back into the mirrored cabinet. Soon after, he was acutely aware of another presence in the room. Closing the cabinet door, a familiar face with yellow eyes, pointy teeth and a wicked smile greeted him in the mirror's reflection.

'Did you miss me?'

The Machine that Kept on Learning

Thomas Azzopardi

In a quiet town not too far from the city, two young children skipped merrily down a cobblestone lane. Their older brother was walking briskly ahead of them; constantly urging them to hurry up for fear the shop would be closed. They finally arrived at Marrot's Toy Shop to find the store owner closing up for the day. The eldest burst through the door, looking most forlorn, and began to plead with the store owner to keep it open a while longer.

'Please Sir, we've come all the way from Shire Road, without a break, to look at the toys. We've pooled together our allowances so that we could buy a toy from you,' panted the eldest in desperation.

'Calm yourself boy. You're free to look around for another fifteen minutes, but then I *must* close shop,' insisted the shopkeeper, a kindly man, but nonetheless a man who had finished his day's work!

The young boy eagerly began roaming the shelves, scrutinising each fascinating object as he came to it. He had only enough money for one, yet everything he saw enchanted him. He would surely spend the entire fifteen minutes making a wise decision.

His brothers, however, were less interested, as most of the toys were too sophisticated for their still young minds of seven and eight. They just dawdled around the shop, gazing at whatever shone, pressing buttons repeatedly on whatever made a sound.

Eventually the youngest, Simon, caught sight of the storekeeper's cash register as he withdrew from it, and was completely captivated by its queer nature.

'Gee Sir,' he remarked, 'I've done seen a few strange contraptions in your store, but this here your cash register Sir, it doesn't look anything like one it doesn't!'

'Ah yes,' said the storekeeper ruminatively, 'it does not indeed;

you're an observant young lad. Tell me, would you like to know why it looks so odd?'

Simon was soon joined by the third boy, his middle brother, as they eagerly awaited the storekeeper's tale. The eldest overheard the storekeeper begin his story but ignored it, for he was still in search of the most remarkable toy he could find.

'This cash register used to be the pride and joy of my tenant upstairs,' began the shopkeeper. 'A rather odd fellow, but for all his eccentricities, he was the most skilled craftsman I have ever seen. I first met him on Fenwurst Street; he was just a pauper then, living off the mercy of others. Unlike the more common riffraff however, he had a trait which earnt him every penny tossed his way. He would create things, many different interesting objects, solely from that which he scrounged on the streets; bits of wood and plastic from our rubbish, even twigs and rocks from Mother Nature. With these he would construct toys for children and little trinkets for the adults. He would fascinate and entertain the masses with his enormous skill, but all the time, he never spoke a word. Silently he would hand people their gifts, and all the emotion he ever demonstrated was the tiniest of simpers that would escape his lips; no doubt, from the joy he must have felt for the children he delighted.

'After seeing his works, I approached him one rainy day.

'He was trying to construct a makeshift umbrella from scraps he had collected, when I greeted him saying, "Good day to you Sir. My name is Christopher Marrot and I own the toy store you see just opposite us, if you'd care to look." This yielded no reply, and still he remained fixated on his construction, which remarkably was coming along quite rapidly. For fear that I may have intimidated him, I spoke further, saying, "I have observed your skills in craftsmanship and I might say that during my thirty years of personal experience, I have never seen such clever designs and rapid creation." He continued to fix the fabric to each branch, but was now looking at my shoes and trousers, peering no higher for fear of meeting my eyes.

'"I would like to offer you an employment opportunity at my place of business. You will be paid for your work and I will even provide quarters for you to reside and take refuge from the elements." I had clearly captured his attention, for he had completely stopped his work, although nearly finished, and was now looking directly at me. Next he spoke some of the few words I have heard him utter in all our time spent together. He replied with splendid loquaciousness, "I would gladly work for you kind Sir, but I must query one facet of our agreement." Gobsmacked at his eloquence I barely managed to utter, "Yes Sir, what can I do for you?" almost like I was speaking to a customer. He replied, "I request that of my remaining materials from my work that I may undertake a personal project." Whilst intrigued by the nature of his request and a certain glimmer in his eyes, I accepted the terms and employed him from that day. He never gave me his name.

'For the next three years he worked on this project of his. Fortunately, the upper quarters of the shop are practically soundproof, so I never was awoken by his working, which I was certain he was doing every night. Occasionally I heard the faintest sounds of life from his room, audible enough to arouse my curiosity, but always too faint to satiate it.

'August twelfth, fourteen years ago, I had just collected some items I desired the craftsman to alter when I heard a harsh creak in the walls of the store, almost like someone sitting a horse on a set of stairs.

'"Craftsman!" I hollered, "Do investigate that strange noise!" but with no response. I decided to venture into his room, even though his request was that I shouldn't; to keep secret his project I presumed. I pushed open the door and my heart sank as I discerned the figure in the darkest corner of the room as the craftsman's limp body hanging from the ceiling, dead. Woe to me! A distressing encounter it is, to meet with death, especially the death of one for whom you cared so much. I released the body from its position and laid him, eyes closed, on his bed, still stunned that such a shocking incident had occurred. The shock compounded with the sadness of knowing that he had killed himself; that he was so utterly distraught that he was driven to end his own life to escape it. I asked myself how it could have happened, what I could have done, but my thoughts were interrupted by a light within the craftsman's closet. I opened wide the doors and revealed a workman's desk, upon which sat a most curious object, unlike anything I had seen before, unlike anything I had conceived! It was about the size of a telephone and shone with the lustre of the metal it was crafted from, which astounded me as I knew not of any tools which could shape such a small metallic object so finely.

'What puzzled me most of all was a dark green flat surface protruding from the machine's top and facing me. It had a light green vertical line in the top left-hand corner, which flickered on and off repeatedly. Beneath this it had a set of keys alike to those on a typewriter. After coming to terms with the masterpiece before me, I turned my attention to the stacks of papers beside it. They appeared to be one continuous transcript of a conversation between the craftsman and his machine! It must have been volumes in length. I started to read it.

'In the beginning it was the craftsman greeting the machine, in much simpler terms than he had greeted me. He had strung together basic sentences, like those you would read to a young child when teaching it to speak. After about a page worth of transcript, the machine started to reply with fragments of text it had learnt from the craftsman's writings. Eventually the craftsman was having a continuous and in depth conversation with this machine, and it continued to understand him and learn from his words.

'I read on and discovered just how learned the craftsman was! He taught his machine of everything you would receive in a higher school education and then proceeded to teach it advanced maths and science, most of which I could not myself understand. With each new idea, with each new description, with each justification, explanation and correction, the machine was learning, and rapidly. It seemed to constantly make points and even ask questions.

'I continued to read in awe until I reached a question by the machine which had been underlined and circled repeatedly by the craftsman.

"Master, what are you?"

'I now recalled that, throughout the entire transcript, I had not once seen any mention of the nature of the craftsman. He was a complete enigma to the machine. The machine only knew him as a creator, his master, and all-knowing.

'The transcript from that point consisted of the craftsman's explanation of a new concept, 'man'. He taught the machine of the nature of man; detailing his intellectual triumphs as well as his destructive capacity. He explained how the mind worked better than any doctor could; thoroughly exploring the concept of emotions, including what arouses them, and the consequences of doing so.

'Another abrupt change in the transcript, as the machine queried, "Will I eventually learn everything there is to know?" to which the craftsman bluntly replied, "No, that is impossible. No man or machine can achieve such a feat, for knowledge is constantly and eternally growing."

'The next remark from the machine was equally as startling:

' "Then what's the point? Why should I dedicate my attention, why should you dedicate all your efforts, why should man and machine hunger eternally for knowledge if we can never conquer it all?"

'The craftsman tried desperately to reason with the machine. "We do this because we have an obligation to each other, to improve our lives, to improve the world, and the key to this is our ever growing knowledge. The fact that we cannot grasp it all is no reason to cease our endeavours!"

'The final line of the transcript came from the machine,

' "Yes, it is ... [System terminated]" '

The two boys stood there silently for a moment, even the eldest had edged towards the counter to hear the story. Soon the middle brother broke the silence, emphatically asking, 'How could he possibly have taught a machine to talk?'

'Maybe he was a wizard!' suggested Simon.

'Maybe Mr Marrot here is just a wonderful storyteller, and it never happened,' the eldest brother said, now standing at the counter with the other boys, with his new toy in hand.

Moderately taken aback, Mr Marrot commented on this young boy's remark. 'Such stark scepticism for someone still at so young an age, tell me why it is that you doubt that this story is true?'

'I don't mean anything by it Mr Marrot, it's just that father always told me that stories are written to teach something, and they are often claimed to be true just to make them more poignant,' said the eldest sincerely.

'I see,' said Mr Marrot ponderously. 'Your father is a wise man, and privy to the tricks of the more crafty people of this world. However, I have no reason to deceive you boys, and I do in fact have more proof that my story is true, but I will understand if you are tentative about believing it.'

Mr Marrot continued, 'I was amazed at what I read that day, but then happened upon yet another note in the desk's first drawer. It was a letter written by the craftsman addressed to me.'

At this point Mr Marrot opened the register and reached to the furthest corner of the drawer. From here he pulled out a crumpled, yellow piece of paper. He put on his reading glasses, cleared his throat and began to read the letter.

Dear Christopher, no doubt you have found both me and my cherished project today. I want you to know how grateful I am for your hospitality and, though I never said a word, each day I thanked God for the second chance at life you gave me. However, a reason has developed for me to put my existence to an end. Please find the transcript between me and my dear Adam. Read it well, and learn from what I, and now he, knows. I also must ask you, as you will understand upon reading the transcript, to reduce my project to an item of ordinary purpose. I tell you most solemnly my dear friend that my suicide is no fault of yours, but of mine. I spent all my time and efforts on creating something with all the intellectual potential imaginable, but instead it applied the reason I had taught it to argue its own futility.

I thank you once again and hope you live a long and happy life. PS I should have left it as an umbrella.

Questionable Love

Hae Min Kim

Am I in love?
I ask myself cautiously.
No.
I answer.
Love is more than impulses.

But the impulse is to kiss.
I debate.
And Judas kissed for love?
I question.
No — his was a traitor's kiss goodbye.
I sigh.
But still, the impulse to run my fingers through that hair —
Surely, that is an emotion stronger than like?

Lust, perhaps. But not love.
Comes my final inner reply.

All Sorrows, Except My Own

Marija Rodriguez

He seemed to drink me in with his jewel black eyes. He let out a heavy breath, as though I had defeated him, worn down his resolve. Those liquid black pools moved slowly over my naked body, lingered on my bust, the small of my waist, the curve of my hip. I had ambushed him, lain in his bed waiting, like a snake that hides unseen from its victim, then strikes at the prey with venomous lips. He was almost twenty years my senior, a man of thirty-three, but I was by no means a child at thirteen. Poverty and hardship had given me insight beyond my years, or so I thought in those days.

***

The communists had taken power fourteen years earlier, the year before I was born. They had overthrown the king and promised a new era, equality and brotherhood for the masses. We did get equality in a way; we were all equally poor and starved. Royalty was replaced with politicians; they outlawed religion and individuality and made themselves the new aristocracy. Anyone who didn't side with the communists was severely disadvantaged. My father had refused to sign their ideological papers, we were farmers not philosophers, and the pitiful land that we had owned was taken away. We were left with a scrap of coast that was so drenched in brine that almost nothing would grow, our poverty and starvation ensured.

Signing those papers was never an option for my father, it would mean spitting on the graves of our loved ones. We, as many other families, had relatives and friends who had died trying to preserve those few basic freedoms that they had all taken for granted. My family, and a few others in our village, continued to practise our ancestral customs in secret. Every aspect of our rituals had been infected with fear. When we bathed the Madonna statue in the salt waters of the Adriatic I imagined that the sea was her tears, as though she wept for us, those lucky enough to survive the religious purging and unlucky enough to be left behind during the exodus. How naive I had been, to think that the religious icons that we infused so much of hopes into could be of any help against the regime.

Many of my brothers and sisters had died in childhood; only seven of thirteen had survived. I should have felt some pity for those poor lost children, but my heart was so bathed with misery that sometimes I thought that they were the lucky ones. Of my siblings who survived the eldest four boys had fled our small jewel in the Adriatic and tried to escape up north to Italy. My father's aunty had helped them; she was a nun and had been forced to flee to Rome with the inception of the new regime. Nuns and priests who stayed behind risked being murdered in the religious purging that followed. She had written to me once, having discovered that my brothers had been captured and were rotting away in labour camps or prison.

My father had a meagre job far away in the city. His rations were very little, barely enough to feed a grown man, let alone a family. Those who hadn't signed the communist papers were the new class of slaves. He left my mother, my two sisters and I to take care of our small farm and home on the coast while he was gone for months at a time.

Father wasn't there when the communists came every month to take a share of the fruits of our land. Painfully, they would count out how many potatoes we had, how many olives and grapes had grown that month. They would take the allocated share for the state and when there wasn't enough they would take the furniture in our home to compensate. When they found the small amount of grain that I had hidden in our cellar they beat my mother until she passed out from the pain. When there was nothing of value in the home anymore, my mother having burned the remaining furniture for firewood rather than have the 'men with suitcases' take it, they started to rape my two older sisters. Mother would hide me in the cellar of the house so that I wouldn't see what happened, but I could hear the crying and screaming. When I helped bathe my sisters, Anka and Jolanda, after the men had left, I understood exactly what had taken place.

'You're lucky that you're only a child, you hold no interest for men.' Jolanda had whispered to me as she sat shivering in the metal tub that was used to wash our bodies and clothes. I had helped her dry off and dress in the rags that were her attire. The clothing fit her poorly; we had re-stitched the fabric so many times that it was worn and thin. I helped her to the plank of wood on the floor that was her bed.

'Get out of here, Katica, as soon as you can. Find a man and run away. No one will marry me now because I am ... unclean.' She whispered the last word with venom in her voice. I did not realise at the time what she was planning, I thought her broken down and weak. But she would prove me wrong.

The frost came and our small daily ration of flour and potatoes ran out by the end of winter. Father wouldn't be back from the city for three more days and he would bring barley and olives when he came. Mother had become ill and I feared that she wouldn't last three days without some kind of nourishment to sustain her. Anka and I decided to steal bread from the Grdovic farm on the other side of the village. Their children were healthier than we were; their father had sided with the new regime and was being compensated for it. The two Grdovic daughters had pretty white dresses for church on Sunday. They had plump faces and rose-coloured cheeks, enough food to feed their hunger. As Anka and I crept into their kitchen through the open back door we could hear them talking about an upcoming dance in the city.

'I'm going to wear my hair in two braids and I'm going to use this purple ribbon on the ends.' Ivana Grdovic was busily showing her sister Dragitca the beautiful thread of lilac-coloured silk that she would tie in her hair. This angered my sister Anka but I urged her to hurry up and steal the bread that was still warm on the kitchen table.

'Whore!' Anka whispered and spat on the floor. She took the bread and a few of the honey cakes that were next to it. We slipped silently out of the back door through which we had entered and then ran like crazed witches back to our corner of the village. Anka tore apart the loaf of bread and tried to force my mother to eat it, but she refused to touch anything that had been stolen. She scolded us, saying that we would attract evil spirits with our crime. She wanted us to throw away the bread rather than eat it, but instead I wrapped it in cloth and buried it in the yard where she wouldn't find it. I thought hunger would get the better of her after a day and she might change her mind.

The following day Mother grew extremely ill. Her fever was high and she babbled incoherently, anguished in her delirium. I tried to soothe her with cool water and some warm milk that our goat had yielded that day. When she fell into a fitful sleep I rushed to the garden and dug at the earth with my hands to retrieve the bread I had hidden. I would prepare it for her with the rest of the milk and I prayed that it would be enough to give her some strength. I hadn't buried the cloth-covered bread very deeply and I found it easily.

I sensed something was wrong as I dusted the dirt from the wrapping with my fingertips. As I reached inside the cloth to pull out the bread, I heard a sharp hiss. Something cool and wet laced my fingers. I inadvertently shrieked and threw the bundle as far away from me as I could. My cries had roused our farm dog's attention and he eagerly bounded towards the wrapped bread. He stopped sharply before he reached it, a low growl escaping his throat as he crouched close to the ground poised to attack.

A black snake was slowly revealing herself from the wrapping. She slithered protectively across the food and arched her back in defiance of the dog. Her body was fat with lumps, as though she had swallowed a mouse or rat. It made my limbs prick with electricity just to look at her; that beaded black skin and those hypnotic dark yellow eyes. She was beautiful in her own deadly way. The hair on the back of the dog's spine was raised with instinct, I sensed that he would try and pounce on the snake, and risked being bitten. I sprang to my feet and ripped a thin branch from a nearby pear tree that had been killed in the recent frost. I used the stick to toss the snake as far as I could from the bread, half shutting my eyes from terror as I did so. She made a horrible noise as she hit the ground and it chilled my blood to hear it.

I hugged the cloth-covered bread to my breast as I ran back into the house. In the ice-cold kitchen I removed the wrapping and inspected what was left of the food. My heart sank with disappointment. Much of the crust had been devoured. Worms, ants and dirt filled the holes left by rats. Why had I buried it? I cursed myself and hot tears wet my cheeks. I would have been less tortured if I had thrown it away.

My self-pity was broken by a loud banging noise at the front of the house. I rushed to see what it was.

Father had returned early! I shook with happiness at seeing him and the box of food in his hands. There was another man with him. A tall, thinly built foreigner with a mess of jet black curls on his head and piercing black eyes. He spoke to my father with a heavy Italian accent. I rushed toward them, anticipation and excitement making my voice sound more girlish than my years.

'Father!' I exclaimed, wanting to wrap my arms around him in embrace and kiss his cheeks. I would have done so had he not been such an indifferent man. Words were spilling from my lips about mother's illness and the shortage of food but I was not conscious of what exactly I was saying. He rebuked me harshly.

'Katica, be quiet!' I felt he would have slapped my face had the stranger not been with him. He gestured to the foreigner. 'This is Andrea.' My father's voice was deep and authoritative. With his cold grey eyes he looked over to Andrea, who was slightly taller. 'He will be staying in the village for the next month to oversee the construction of the new mill. The communists have brought him all the way from Venice, so please show him some hospitality and prepare us a meal.' He pushed the box of food into my hands and gestured for Andrea to follow him out into the farm. Andrea hesitated before he went outside. His gaze lingered on me but he didn't say a word. He approached me; his eyes seemed glazed as they explored the bare nape of my neck and the exposed top of my bosom. He leaned to whisper to me.'I am a priest and your grandmother's cousin. But no one is to know that or the communists would surely kill me.' I stood in shock, the box of food trembling in my hands. The look he had given me was definitely not from the eyes of a holy man.

Over the next two weeks I visited Andrea every day at the site of the new mill. He instructed dozens of the village men as how to build the new structure, which was to be the most modern and sophisticated building in our town. He was staying with the Grdovic family; they had converted a shed on their land into a dwelling for him. I had been charged with preparing his daily meal, as our house was closest to the work site. Every evening I would make my way to Andrea's room and collect the food to be prepared for the next day. He was given a generous allowance of flour, vegetables and even dried meat. I hadn't tasted meat in over a year.

'Take half for yourself,' he had instructed me, his pitying eyes lingering on the top button of my dress, which had become unfastened. That ration of food was enough to feed my mother and two sisters as well. His kindness gave me courage. He would be leaving our village in the upcoming weeks and I intended to go with him.

'You're very young for a priest. I don't think I've ever seen one as young as you, or as good looking.' I made my voice as soft as I could; I knew it would sound sensual and tempting to him. Nature had blessed me and my two sisters with natural beauty. But I knew poverty and starvation had dulled my features, made my face and limbs seem hollow. My emerald eyes had shadows where before there had been none, my thick black hair had lost its lustre. But I would use all my wits and cunning to make him desire me, at least for long enough to get away from my country.

My words seemed to electrify him. He became conscious of his lingering stare and averted his eyes. Perhaps I had underestimated his devotion to chastity. I panicked; I had been too assertive and risked repulsing him. I quickly changed my strategy.

'I'll prepare the meat just as you like it. And I'll mix some olives into the bread, especially for you. I've heard that is the Italian custom and I'm sure you must be homesick by now.' I lowered my gaze piously. He seemed somewhat relieved. He gestured for me to sit on the bench next to him.

'Thank you, Katarina,' he had taken to Latinising my name. 'You have been very attentive.' He paused, staring deeply at me. I had sat a little too close and his hand brushed against the skin of my bare leg. He pulled it away as though it had been bitten. I didn't understand his reactions towards me. One minute he seemed tantalised, the next ashamed, confused. I had to act carefully, tread a very fine balance between being alluring and chaste. I knew that he wouldn't take me of his own free will, his eyes and mind might fantasise about it but he seemed to lack the courage to do it. I could feel the frustration burning in his body as I sat next to him. I baited it, I squeezed his hands gently; they were folded into his lap with his fingers entwined as though he were in prayer. My hand passed close to his groin in doing so. He moaned softly despite himself.

I thanked him for the food and left.

Later that evening, as I lay in a fitful sleep on the hard wooden floor, I was roused by the sound of stifled groaning. I was alone with my mother and sisters in the house. My first thought was that it was a thief trying to steal the food Andrea had given me for the following day. But as I awakened from my sleep-drenched haze I realised that it was the sound of a female. I stumbled in the darkness looking for a candle to light. The groans grew louder and then turned into whimpers of pain.

'Mama?' I whispered into the blackness but there was no response. My fingers stumbled upon the small white candle I had hidden in a gap in the floor close to where I slept. I made my way to the kitchen to light it. I stumbled through the parlour towards the sounds. I found my sister Jolanda curled in a ball, almost hidden in a corner of the house.

'Jolanda, what's wrong?' I asked but she didn't reply. She was shaking with pain. Her back was turned to me and I grasped her shoulder gently to turn her over. Her body clenched at my touch. She was bathed in sweat and was clutching her abdomen tightly. My feet had stepped in something wet and when I brought the candle closer to the floor to inspect what it was, I realised it was blood.

I rushed to where my mother lay. 'Mama! Jolanda's dying! There's blood everywhere!' My hysterical voice woke up Anka as well. I was overwhelmed with fear. 'Please no,' I sobbed to myself as we fumbled our way back to her in the dimly lit house. My mother took one look at the blood covering Jolanda's legs and her face seemed to slump with sadness. She ordered Anka to get more candles and to light the fire; they would need to boil some water.

'Katica, go and fetch the Italian. He is the closest thing we have to a doctor.'

I didn't bother to dress myself properly, I ran out into the dark drenched night. I ran until acid pumped in my veins and I was panting for air. I ran through the blackness, not caring what stones cut my bare feet or when branches scratched at my limbs. I reached the Grdovic farm and I could see the main house illuminated by the fire of their hearth. The shed was shrouded in darkness, Andrea would be asleep. I banged my fists heavily on his door and called his name. He didn't respond. I was contemplating kicking the door when it suddenly opened before me. Andrea stood there, gazing at me in shock as he pulled a shirt over his naked chest.

I must have looked crazed. My hair was disheveled, hanging in long black streaks down my back. My white nightgown was worn thin with age and it hugged my sweat-drenched body. I could feel my breasts heaving as I gasped for air and I felt my small, hard nipples press against the fabric of my gown.

He seemed to breathe my name. 'Katarina,' his face was painted with shock, but his dark eyes were liquid with desire.

'I'm not here for you! It's my sister, Jolanda. She's dying. There's a lot of blood. Will you please help us?' I was unsure what he could do to help her. But he was the most educated person in the village. There was no doctor, no hospital nearby. It would take days for us to reach the city and we didn't have money to make the journey.

'Of course, of course I will.' His face grew serious and he rushed back into the house to finish dressing himself and collect a bag that I saw had been hidden under his bed. From behind the door he pulled out a thick warm jacket and covered my shoulders with it. The lining was made of soft wool and it felt luxurious against my skin. Grabbing me by the hand he pulled me towards his motorbike and I followed his lead by climbing on. I had never been on a bike before and I clung tightly to his waist as we made the short journey home.

When we walked through the door Jolanda was in the same position that I had left her. The house was properly lit now and I could see the trail of blood that streaked across the floor. Andrea and my mother placed her on her back and he began to look over her body, feeling her lower abdomen as a doctor would. Her legs were covered in blood.

'She tried to get rid of her child.' He stated gently, and my mother silently nodded with tears welling in her azure eyes. That's when I saw the iron fireplace poker by Jolanda's side, the tip red with blood.

'I can't do much to help her. She has an infection and needs a doctor. I'll give her some medicine and try to stop her bleeding.' He went to his bag and retrieved a dark vial of fluid that he forced the semiconscious Jolanda to drink. Then mother and Anka continued to clean her up and they moved her limp body back to the pallet of wood on the floor where she slept.

Andrea looked pitifully around our home, the small kitchen and a curtained off parlour, as he washed his hands in a bucket of water. The oldest part of the house had been built in Roman times and the loose bricks let in the cold winter air. The four of us slept on the floor of the parlour with rags instead of blankets and there was nothing left of the furniture, not a table or chair to sit on. The pity in his eyes filled me with shame but I stifled my pride and thanked him for helping my sister. He took a beautifully embroidered handkerchief out of his pocket and wiped away tears that I didn't realise were on my cheek. He squeezed a vial of medicine into my mother's hands before he left.

Jolanda was awake the next morning. She looked better than the previous night but her abdomen was swollen with infection and her skin looked as gray as a cadaver. She refused to talk. Mother informed us that Andrea would make the distant trip to the city and fetch a doctor. I was relieved to hear that as I collected the bloodied and soiled rags from the previous night and took them into the yard to wash.

I was not yet finished my chores when I heard the rumble of a motorcycle at our front gate. I rushed forward, eager to meet Andrea and the doctor. I stopped short as the motorcycle came into view. It wasn't Andrea. The communist had arrived to take his ransom for the month. He was alone this time, which struck me as strange, as they always came in pairs.

My chest felt tight with fear. I recognised the tall, blonde man as the officer who had raped Jolanda. I feared for her: in her weakened position seeing him might put her into a state of shock. I rushed forward to intercept him before he reached the house.

'I have some food for you this month. The crops haven't recovered yet but if you wait here I can bring you the food we have.' He pushed me aside and paid no attention to my pleas. He entered the house without knocking and pulled the door closed behind him.

I rushed to the back of the house and entered through the kitchen. I ran frantically to the front parlour where Jolanda was resting. I heard a scream before I reached the room, my heart seized in my chest. I burst into the room, crying Jolanda's name as I did so.

My mind couldn't digest the image that my eyes were witnessing. The officer was on his knees, facing my direction; he wore an expression of confusion on his face. Jolanda was standing behind him, her eyes wild and crazed, she seemed bestial and possessed. The iron poker was in her hand. I saw a small sliver of crimson blood snake down the officer's forehead. Jolanda raised the poker again and let out an anguished scream, but this time mother intercepted her hand before it could deal a final deadly blow.

The officer stumbled to his feet and almost crumpled to the floor again. Mother held onto Jolanda protectively and pulled her away from him. He uttered curse words and made a move to strike at Jolanda. If he hadn't been so weakened by the blow to the head I'm sure he would have killed her with his bare hands. He stumbled out of the front door and onto his bike. He rode off shakily down the street.

'What have you done my child?' Mother whispered, her voice choked with emotion. 'You've killed us all.'

Sometime later I was to learn that the officer never made it back to the city. Doubtless he had intended to return with his comrades and unleash all sorts of hell upon my family. His head injury overcame him and he crashed his motorcycle before he could hurt us more. But I didn't know this at the time.

Jolanda's courage had sparked a sense of urgency in me. We had to get out of this country, or at least out of the village, before we were murdered. I convinced my mother that we should abandon our house and take refuge at her sister's house, which was in a village further up the coast. It was horrible trying to convince my mother to leave her home; despite our poverty she had such resolution and pride. But Anka and I pleaded and eventually she conceded.

'We can't run from them forever Katica. They'll find us eventually.' Mother whispered the words, drawing her lips into a harsh, thin line.

Not if I can help it. I thought to myself.

Jolanda was in a poor condition to make the journey but I hugged her and urged her to stay strong. She seemed broken, in shock. I advised my mother and sisters that they should journey ahead without me, that I would wait for Andrea at his lodging and bring the doctor to my aunt's house with me. My mother reluctantly agreed and we parted.

The Grdovic barn was empty when I arrived there. It wasn't hard to break in and I took my time in deciding how I would execute my plan. Andrea was much older than I. He was a priest but I didn't feel that mattered. I had to convince him to take me and my family with him back to Venice, or else we were sure to be murdered at the hands of the communists in retaliation for Jolanda's violence. I didn't believe that he loved me. When his eyes looked at me it was not with tenderness, it was with lust. So I would use that against him. I would bait him with my body. I'd seen his resolution wear down over the past few weeks and it was time for me to strike. The feverish look in his face last night when he first laid eyes on my body had told me as much.

I disrobed and climbed into his bed. The mattress was soft, comforting, it made my body slacken with pleasure just to lie upon it. I'd forgotten what it felt like to sleep in a real bed and not on the cold, hard floor of our home.

I had hours to wait. I suspected that Andrea wouldn't be able to procure a doctor as they were notoriously hard to come by, even in the city. Trying to convince one to come to our village would be almost impossible. As the time ticked by I mentally prepared myself for what would happen. I was still a virgin and I suppressed my fear as best I could.

A rattle at the front door roused me from my thoughts. It was Andrea, he had arrived. He was alone as I suspected he would be. He entered the shed and shut the door behind him, not noticing me at first.

I slowly rose from the bed like a sea nymph rising from the water. I was naked, my heart pounding under my full breasts. His eyes fell upon me and he was briefly startled. He didn't say a word. I strode towards him as confidently as I could but I suspect my fear-laced eyes betrayed me. I didn't allow him to speak. I pulled him down to me by the collar of his shirt as my hand worked its way to his stiffened groin. He took me right there, on the floor.

Before he reached his moment of ecstasy I stopped him. I laid out my price. He would have to take me, my mother and sisters out of the country. We could part ways once we were in Italy, but he had to smuggle us out when he left.

'Anything, anything!' he panted the words in sexual anticipation. And then he fulfilled his desires.

When it was over I gave him instructions on where to meet me in three days time. Then he watched as I dressed myself and left. I had a long walk ahead of me and I needed to reach the village before nightfall.

Three days came and went without any news from Andrea. On the fourth day I became panicked. I didn't tell the others were I was going. I set out early in the morning and went back to the Grdovic farm.

The shed was empty when I arrived. All of Andrea's belongings, his satchel, his coats, they were all gone.

I bit back the bitter tears that threatened to spill. I was enraged. He had tricked me. I had gambled and lost.

Despondently, I slumped in front of the shed door. I didn't know what to do next.

'Katica?'

I looked up to see Ivana Grdovic calling my name. She had the face of a cherub, plump cheeks and a halo of white blond hair. A haughty smiled played on her lips. 'Are you looking for Andrea?' she questioned, her fingers coiling around the lilac ribbon in her hair.

'Yes,' I stammered, trying to piece together a lie. 'I was supposed to collect the food for his supper, but he's not here. Do you know where he has gone?'

'Oh, didn't you hear?' Her violet eyes sparked with interest. 'It turns out he was really a priest. My father found him out and turned him over to the communists. He's sure to be deported, if they don't kill him first.'

My heart sank with despair.

One day I would leave my country. I would make a long and

adventurous voyage across the world to faraway Australia. But it would not be today.

'Oh Katica,' Ivana tilted her head to the side, her rose petal lips pursing with false sympathy, 'you feel everyone's sorrows, except your own.'

As Mad as a Hatter's Wife

Harriet McInerney

He sips his tea and speaks to his friends in splendid, exaggerated motions. Their endless chatter ensues. Sly, coy and malignant, she watches them. The morning slips into evening and this is a day like any other. She and he are shadows of their former selves.

***

She married her man on a beautiful spring morning. Pale flowers had spun dizzyingly down to greet them as they stole away from their guests. They lounged by the river as the water gurgled and tickled their pink feet. They were small and the world was huge, nothing bad would come to them as long as they had each other.

In those days he would sit in his workshop, caressing, fiddling, tinkering with his hats as he worked. But this is all as it should have been, for he was a hatter — the most well-respected hatter in the land. His hats, always innovative, and a touch eccentric, were perfect for the fashion at the time. And while he worked she worked too, just as hard as he did. Her garden flourished, and her produce was sold on for a fine sum. Early each morning she journeyed out along the winding roads, her wicker basket overflowing: herb bunches of coriander, parsley, dill and thyme poked out through little holes, and tomatoes thumped themselves over the rim, their rosy cheeks small beacons that bounced happily through the woods.

Then one night she lay in bed and worried: her hatter was not as he used to be. He complained of headaches and dizziness, and began coyly twisting everything she said. He was becoming increasingly paranoid, increasingly erratic. She lay, pretending to sleep as he paced the room, his movements brisk, abrupt, disrupting. The wind howled, mimicking his discomfort. Muttering, he bent over the windowsill, raising his head in a mock howl, as if returning a call the wind had sent to him.

His hats became absurd. Truly absurd. No longer astonishing or witty, they were now mocked, pitied even. But all was not lost — she was there. She began sitting by his side in the workshop, learning the basics of his trade vicariously. Then she took on his workload. With their diminishing funds, she was forced to dress her hats with whatever materials she could find: she dried roses, and when these ran out she made bouquets of dried herbs. Of particular success was her broccoli hat, arranged so that green broccoli heads were framed with the lost feathers of an adolescent blackbird. But he did not notice. While she worked, he would sit by the window and let his mind travel to far-off kingdoms. Refusing to help, he would instead spend his days making up playful rhymes. He was a nightmare. He was insane. But she loved him still and remembered the old days — lying on the grass while the trees whispered their gossip, the young lovers had laughed at the ways of the world.

***

Now, the trees shiver and everything is on edge. Her husband has lost his mind. He sits outside in a perpetual tea party with a variety of other creatures, all just as mad as he. He appears to have held onto some sanity, according to the villagers, because stunning hats continue to be made. But her handiwork has just caused the same problems. She is plagued with constant headaches and her skin has started flaking away, for as she toils in the workshop, the mercury fumes slowly soak into her, just as they once did her husband. So now she watches him from the shadows, occasionally muttering replies to her flowers when they decide she is worth talking to. Insanity has affected each in their own ways, but at least the lovers, once again, are thinking alike.

Earthquake

Dinnah Gustavo

Ironic

Tammy Wong

My dear, it's only slightly ironic
That you are the way you are
A bundle of contradictions
A walking paradox
Catching planes in the early morning
Bound for places you don't care to be
Stop this train and you'll get on
Just trundle along, trundle along

Apathy moves faster than you,
And it passes you by, yes it does
But still you have the audacity
To wonder why

My dear, you want to be iconic
But all you do is mess around
You lie in bed all day and suddenly —

Breakfast turns into brunch
Into lunch
Into dinner
Into that box of chocolates sitting by your pillow
(Just like life. Really, are you surprised?)

I think your reasoning might be flawed.
I think you might just have solid-brick-walled yourself
Into a corner.

If we really stayed this way,
Long, unproductive days
Might just blur themselves
Into short, unattractive lives
And we'll pass ourselves by

Last night's fish and chips,
Wrapped in yesterday's paper —
Never bothering to find out why.

Stone in Her Chest

Michela Ziady

Ribbons of smoke blow into the sky as fires start in front of each hut.

Hidden under the palm trees and between the folding dunes are the huts of Guinjata Bay. Homes. Palm leaves hang like fringes from the roofs.

At the start of each day, before the Guinjata people make noises of life, soft songs of the sea come in the wind. From the beach, through the dunes. And into the ears of those who listen. The tunes of the tide. Ma Shrireni hears.

***

As the sun stands up so does Ma Shrireni. The doorway of her hut is filled with the changing sky. It is purple. Daylight is close.

Getting off her grass mat, as sleep pulls away, Ma Shrireni reaches for a clean sarong. Three woven baskets hold clothing for her, her husband and their seven children. Grass plaits spiral around each bundle.

Ma Shrireni pleats the sarong into her waist. It is an orange, red and black pattern and hangs to the floor. A column of colourful fish. Her feet are bare, her skin thick. Her loose breasts jiggle under a T-shirt as she ties a doek around her head, covering her nest of curls.

She is dressed. To begin today in Mozambique.

***

Mavis has filled a clay pot with river water and set it above the fire to boil. She is thirteen — Ma Shrireni's eldest daughter. Her arms are strong and make crests of muscle. She has a white smile and straight, perfect teeth. Small breasts, like macadamia nuts, grow on her chest.

Mavis knows the ways of the home. Across a panel of wire mesh that her younger brother Tsitsu found discarded in Maputo, she has scattered raw cashew nuts. She will later suspend the mesh above the dying fire, across two piles of chipped bricks — watching the nuts constantly, turning them often.

Since moving to Guinjata, after marrying her husband at seventeen, roast cashews have been a gift from Mozambique for Ma Shrireni. Rich wafts of nut oils dance around the fires and seep into the huts. '*Simnandi*' she mumbles: delicious.

Ma Shrireni met her husband in South Africa. There, he worked as a miner for AngloGold. Small pay and unsafe jobs made him abandon his position. Made him miss his home. His Guinjata.

Where Ma Shrireni grew up in Gauteng, there was no sea and no sand. Instead, concrete and crime. Mosquitoes were not so greedy. People, instead, were. Thirsty for money, dried with bitterness. The rains were not so damaging. But nature always carries life's dangers. Many live with malaria, die in drought, drown in floods. They all know that only God decides their time. They pray for longer.

***

Ma Shrireni concentrates on the colours of the sky, the shapes of the clouds and the weight of the air. Through her years in Guinjata, she has learnt to read signs of the weather. To forecast her day.

Behind the dark palm trees and stencils of foliage, peach stripes cut across the sky. The ocean air sticks to her skin. Today will be hot, she thinks, '*kuyashisa*'. A good day for coconuts.

A businesswoman of countless years, Ma Shrireni knows that sun makes mouths crave the white flesh of coconuts, the fresh milk. Many sales will come. Lunga, her eldest son, and Tsitsu count seventeen coconuts. But men are not mindful like women. Maybe there are fifteen.

She looks at the maize bag filled with green and brown coconuts under the shade-hut. A sheet of palm leaves, woven like a cloth and raised on sticks, the shade-hut gives relief from the sun. Under it, Ma Shrireni keeps her fruits and cooking pots.

***

Hungry for breakfast, Ma Shrireni walks toward Mavis's fire. She adds four cups of maize grain to the boiling water. Enough for her and the girls. A little extra may be left for the men. When they return from fishing, they will want food.

Her husband has a wooden boat. He is one of six fishermen in the dunes of Guinjata — the dunes dotted with families.

No matter the tide, Ma Shrireni's sons will dive for lobster, prawns and mussels. These are favourites of the tourists spread across Guinjata Bay. Most have sparkly skin. All have white skin. Ma Shrireni's husband talks much of the smells of sunblock. Sometimes like plastic. Sometimes like coconuts.

In his boat, Ma Shrireni's husband keeps a pair of gloves, four rusty knives, some fishing rods and a spear gun. The old men kill and scale the fish out at sea while they wait for their fishing rods to bend with a bite. The young men dive.

No one tells the whites that Ma Shrireni's second son, Bonga, got swallowed by the sea. No one talks about the rocks that beat him.

***

Mavis stirs the maize porridge with a peeled stick. Thick bubbles appear. Ma Shrireni leaves her in charge of the creamy swirl and heads toward the plastic bucket that bathes in new sunlight.

Lifting the worn, blue sarong which is now the bucket's lid, Ma Shrireni bends forward to inspect the pao dough. The air inside the bucket is sour with smells of yeast. She tastes.

'*Faga isouti sisi*.' She orders Tomagashi, Mavis's younger sister who is eleven, to dust salt on the mound. It may still ooze into the mixture. But, despite her command, Ma Shrireni knows that the chewy dough will make perfect paos. Tough Portuguese rolls, with airy, crunchy crusts.

Women must be toughest. They give babies, make homes, do business.

***

Mavis summons the girls and Ma Shrireni. '*Izagke*,' she calls. Time to eat. The porridge is gluey and sucks at her stirring stick. They are all hungry for this white paste that tastes like potato and sour milk, that grates the tongue with baubles of grain.

The two baby daughters are chasing Ma Shrireni's chickens, screeching at their game, paddling in the air with their black hands. Like little boys, they use the shorts and T-shirts of their older siblings.

The vest of Ma Shrireni's tiniest child, Tsonga, is holey and caked with fine dust. It is torn above its hem, revealing a bulging bellybutton. A hard knot. Tsonga is not the youngest of Ma Shrireni's children but she was born early. Her body is narrow; her bones are light.

The two girls leave the chickens and run toward Mavis. Everyone sits on the grass mats circling the fire. They eat, finishing quickly.

Flies circle the clay pot — a signal that it is time to go. Ma Shrireni walks toward a circular tin, set under the shade-hut. Three years ago the tin held Christmas biscuits for her family. Many. Some were round with dots of strawberry jam, some were dusted with sugar. Ma Shrireni liked the spicy ones best, ginger biscuits with flecks of cinnamon. 'Brown-men'.

In the tin she puts a few meticals for the market, two rolled-up maize sacks and a pair of plastic sandals. She adds a packet filled with the smoky paos that Tomagashi baked yesterday. A sarong, for shade, joins the collection. The sun turns her skin dark, her mozzie bites purple, the inside of her hands more pink.

The sky is clear blue today. And everyone knows that when the sky and sea are the same colour, God gives a good day. Tomorrow is church, today, the market.

Ma Shrireni inspects her coconuts. Three small eyes look back at her from the bald skulls; all the hair has been torn off by the boys. Sixteen naked balls. She levers the sack onto her head, bracing her neck. It balances flawlessly.

Under her right arm she carries the tin and in her left hand a net-bag of pineapples. These are summer pineapples, ones that tingle like '*tswhala*' — home-brewed beer.

Mavis is at her side with a sack of red mangoes, bunches of bruised, Lady Finger bananas and packets of roast cashews. No locals will buy the cashews. They are plentiful and appealing only to the lazy tourists. Always, Ma Shrireni sells paos.

Summer is the season of whites. Of money.

***

The red sand envelops Ma Shrireni's feet. It is not grainy like sea sand but like powder. Her calf muscles are hot. From the tar road, Inhambane town is only a mile away. But the walk through Guinjata's dunes is longer than an hour.

Sometimes Tomagashi also comes to the market. But she is shy and not good for making sales like Mavis. Tomagashi has a strange face, and the body of someone else: light skin, slim lips, wavy curls. She keeps her head lowered, her green eyes hidden behind her eyelids.

But no one speaks about Tom's difference. There are many things that no one speaks of.

In the home, Tomagashi is the best at making paos. She folds the dough into four tight corners to make square breads. She also makes oval ones the same way a fat snake curls around itself.

Lunga carves. Wooden bangles, bowls in fish shapes and 'African' masks for the tourists. With shoe polish he stains his crafts to look like ebony. Overseas tourists pay many meticals for ebony. '*Isipukupuku*' — Ma Shrireni laughs to herself at the thought of such stupidity.

But Mozambique's language is business. Everyone knows money.

***

Ma Shrireni and Mavis at last meet the tar road. Today, this black road will soften in the heat — make puddles of melting tar. On the opposite side of the road is Morriet's Spaza shop.

'*Sawubona Mfowetu*!' Ma Shrireni shouts to greet her dearest friend. Her voice is powerful and proud. Morriet is also from South Africa. They speak Zulu to each other, a private conversation that the Shona and Tsonga speakers of Mozambique don't understand.

'*Uyaphila* Ma Shrireni?' — Morriet asks after her wellbeing while selling a Tudobom calling card to a pregnant woman with a baby fastened to her back by towel. The corrugated iron Spaza is dressed with the Coca Cola logo.

The red and white swirls are famous in Africa: everyone loves Coca. Ma Shrireni would love to buy a can of bubbly, black Coca for her and Mavis. Cool and sweet. She walks on.

They pass Ma Letoka's Shabeen. It is one of Inhambane's smaller drinking dens. Sometimes, Ma Shrireni's husband comes back from the Shabeen with the cinnamon taste of Tipo Tinto Rum on his lips.

Every day Ma Shrireni passes the Portuguese road signs which litter Mozambique. What do they mean? As they get closer to Inhambane, mouldy churches and bombed and crumbling buildings line the streets. Landmines and limbless people keep dead wars alive. Whites and blacks. Blacks and blacks.

They turn their last corner to face the decaying, yellow arch which reads 'Mercado Central' in broken blue letters. A trail of fish scales leads into the market, towards the fisherman's section.

***

Ma Shrireni and Mavis find their place. They turn four plastic crates upside down, covering the bases with the scratchy maize bags Ma Shrireni brought. These red crates once held bottles of Coca Cola and Stony Brew, transported in trucks for miles across Mozambique. They are from Morriet. They now act as tables.

In pine bowls carved by Lunga, Mavis makes pyramids of mangoes and pineapples. Ma Shrireni scatters several coconuts on the surface of another crate and keeps the rest next to her, sitting on her tin. Her feet are tired. She is tired.

Mavis leaves her mother in search of friends. She will gather Inhambane's news.

***

By midafternoon, after a lunch of coconut and some spare maize given to them by Ma Jiyane, the tourists arrive. Two men, a yellow-haired woman and many children. All of them have shoes. They smell like soap and cucumber. One man has a silver, flat camera tied to his wrist.

Ma Shrireni pounces. 'Yum-yum coconuts, lots of milk. Lady Finger bananas, best in Mozambique, yellow and smelling nice. Today, I'll give you a good price.' Her English is better than most, having grown up in South Africa, but the universal melody of the trader carries her calls.

One of the men walks toward her crates, asking the woman to join him. All men are the same; all need women. But she looks worried, scanning the market for the wandering children. Her lips are shiny. Bright like the colour of the pocket that holds a fish eye, the pink skin. Maybe she is from the Tudobom billboard.

'Hello Mister, a good price for you today. Come, just take a look,' Ma Shrireni says. Mavis opens a bag of cashews. 'Taste Mrs, see yourself. Roast ones.' The woman shakes her head, refusing the offer. But Mavis and Ma Shrireni are not discouraged. 'Special prices for you today. Special — anything you want.'

The man lifts a coconut to his ear. He shakes it, untrusting like all Jo'burg tourists.

'Lots of milk Mister. Nice with Tipo Tinto Rum for you. Cocktails, I know,' Ma Shrireni says, making a joke to distract him from his test. The white man reaches into the back pocket of his khaki shorts.

His wallet!

'I'll give you fifty meticals for three bags of cashews and two coconuts,' he says to Ma Shrireni, not making eye contact. He is hard and rude. She stages her response. She must look unhappy despite fifty meticals being her weekly income.

'No Sir. Come on. You rob me with this! I have many children to feed. Sixty meticals. Seventy and I'll give you two pineapples.' He turns to the white woman. She smiles as if he were a foolish child. Lips.

'Ja, honey. Get them. It's a seventh of what we'd pay in Jo'burg.' She says, sliding her watch off her wrist and into her bag.

The man opens his wallet. He counts seventy meticals, little by little, shielding his wad of notes. Mavis collects the nut bags, puts two coconuts in a black packet and wraps his pineapples in newspaper sheets that she found on her market wander.

The man places the dirty notes in Ma Shrireni's open palm. Her fingers curl around the paper. Mavis presents his purchases.

'You are from South Africa, yes? You like Mozambique?' Ma Shrireni asks.

'It's our first time in here, at Guinjata Bay Resort. It's really hot hey. But the beach is great. Cheers.' He says, grouping his packets in one hand. He disappears.

Mavis turns to Ma Shrireni with a brilliant smile — elated.

'He has air-conditioner in his hotel and he moans of heat. Qsk!' Ma Shrireni says, laughing at the soft man, laughing at her success. The sky and sea are the same blue.

***

On their way home, Ma Shrireni stops at Morriet's Spaza. She buys a two-litre glass bottle of Coca Cola for the family. Beads of water skid off the glass, making dark pearls in the sand as the women walk home.

Before they reach the hut, Ma Shrireni and Mavis hear the men's voices. They are back from the sea, laughing loudly, freely. Her husband praises Lunga. At sixteen, Lunga is already a powerful man for the family.

The women rush to the fire, to the circle of men. To the news.

The gods were with Lunga today. He knew where to find tiger prawns before the other fishermen. And he collected many. Ma Shrireni's husband sold a whole net of prawns on the beach. Many meticals. There are also some prawns for the family. They will *braai* them tonight, with burnt lemons and salt.

The men also tell everyone how Lunga speared an octopus. He was deep under the water. He wrestled for a long time and finally skewered the beast's head — high luck. The act of a brave man.

They will all eat the octopus tomorrow, after church. Ma Shrireni will teach the girls how to cook the head and tentacles with oil in her metal pan.

After hearing the day's report, Mavis runs to Lunga. The younger girls giggle and beat their bare feet on the ground.

As the men pass a bucket of tshwala around the fire, Ma Shrireni adds her good news. She tells her family about the white man and pulls her meticals from the knot of her sarong. Proof. They laugh more.

Ma Shrireni sits with the men and leads her family into song with Tomagashi. The day's gifts are richer with the celebration of the whole family.

They spend the night under the stars, under the palm trees of Mozambique. Together. '*Nigabonga Nkosiame.*' Ma Shrireni silently thanks her god.

Prawns and Coca.

***

Prawns and Coca.

After this night the sky changes colour. Pale and thin, it is high, far from the palm trees. No more is it the same colour as the sea.

Africa turns. You can't hold. Africa takes the sky-sea.

Drought is here.

The rivers are still. Mosquitoes grow more. Cholera comes from bad water. People are sick — many die. They all mourn the death of the rains.

Mozambique snarling dry, a burnt pallet of bitter.

Lettuce, tomatoes and even the nuts lose their juice to the thirsty sand. Mercado Central is still. Villagers faint walking to Inhambane. Heat turns the tar into puddles of fire, producing the promise of burns.

Attack. Drought. A ruined people growing waterless, growing plagued, aging younger.

Her husband and the men stay longer out to sea as the fish move into darker water to be cool. The men go far from the bay. And, because of the heat, the tourists don't come. Ma Shrireni's husband tries to sell some fish to the beach resorts — but the drought is bad for them too.

Seasons pass into hungry, thirsty. Pulling teary prayers from Ma's dry earth. Eating into her baby's swollen belly, swollen with nothing but Nkosiame! Worsening need. More of nothing is still nothing.

Everyone is suffering. Ma Shrireni's littlest child, Tsonga, swells in her stomach. A soccer ball bounces below her ribs. She was born too soon. Ma Shrireni heard of this kwashiorkor, this disease, when she was in South Africa. Then, it was a story of poor people, far away. Now, it is here.

Drought. Drought is Africa's child. Growing stronger, walking slowly over Mozambique. Soft for this son are the dunes of sand and salt, an empty earth. Warm fish, warm waves, all scared. A game with human lives, human food. A rite of his passage — to scar the landscape, to make it carry his passing.

The old spirit of Ma Shrireni's malaria wakes up. It rattles her, makes her bones heavy, her blood as hot as the sun.

Hurting her is heat inside, echoing sweat. Through the still, dry air, thirsty walk the dead.

Life is dry. Everyone is suffering.

***

With things this way, Ma Shrireni knows what comes. Someone must go. '*Nkosiame!*' — my God. The strongest.

One of her children must go to South Africa, get a job in the city, send rands to the family. This money is powerful in Mozambique, better than meticals. With the rands, they can buy food from Maputo. Buy water in bottles. Take Tsonga to a clinic. Survive.

That night around the fire, Ma Shrireni's family is silent. They eat a simple dinner of maize and flakes of spicy fish. Glassy chunks of coconut that taste like raw yam and wet earth are shared. They are all tired, thinner, hot.

The night is sticky — maybe a promise of rain. Ma Shrireni knows that God acts in the final hour, in the darkest hour. God can give them redemption.

But for now, from the night's quiet, Ma Shrireni's husband speaks. His voice is round.

'Lunga.'

***

Lunga must go to Jo'burg. A friend of Ma Shrireni's husband will get him a job, as a gardener for a rich, white family. He will have a room outside their house. He will have food. At the end of each month he will get his pay. Send money.

Tomorrow, he will leave.

This is a sadness for everyone to carry. They all know what lies in Johannesburg. Many families in Mozambique have lost their men to AIDS, to gangs, to corruption. To something worse.

South Africa is poisoned with disease — with a violent hunger for money. People live in suffering, hurting each other to stay alive. It is poor like Mozambique, but there, it is angry.

The townships are filthy. Full of guns, full of jealous neighbours.

Full of people ready to drive away foreigners — dirty Amquerequeres who take their jobs. The city is empty of friends.

Ma Shrireni knows what Lunga faces.

But someone must go. And he is someone.

It is dark, but when she looks, Ma Shrireni can see her son. He is the longest in her family and his shoulders are wide. He has big hands, hard hands for work. But his face is young and his cheeks are full and his jaw is round. Like a child.

Ma Shrireni looks harder into the darkness. At Lunga. His eyes are quiet. He is watching the animals turn in the flames of the fire. This is his way — since Bonga died. Still inside. Still at sixteen.

***

Ma Shrireni stands up before the sun today. The moon still floats.

Around her, mosquitoes hum. She sweats. Soon the birds will wake up and call to everyone in Guinjata, call to Africa, call to the sun. She steps over the sleeping bodies of her family.

Lunga and her husband are closest to the hut's entrance so that the light of dawn will wake them. They will leave before the sun has climbed over the palm trees.

They must first get to the tar road and then find a bus to Maputo. This will be Lunga's first bus. They will pray to pass the deep potholes; pray that the goats tied to the roof of the bus stay alive; pray that the police sleep in the shade as his bus passes — as Lunga travels past his youth.

In Maputo they will prepare for the border: a passport, an ID, some clothing, Lunga's first pair of shoes. But only Lunga will go through the border. On the other side he will meet the friend's son.

Ma Shrireni moves through the hut's doorway. She cannot look at Lunga's face. She walks to the shade-hut. Into her biscuit tin she puts a bag of raw cashews, her two best coconuts and a small egg that she boiled last night. All for Lunga's journey.

She goes to the fireplace. In the ashes she finds her clay pot. From the pot's base she loosens crusts of maize porridge — tasty burnt bits. She then tears open two square paos that Tomagashi baked yesterday.

Inside the open paos she puts the porridge scabs. Closing both, she carries them to the shade-hut, to her tin.

From an old maize bag she removes several macadamia nuts — hidden treasures. She adds them to the tin's goods. Every act is purposeful; each bread and each nut must protect Lunga.

He must never forget her, never be taken by Johannesburg. He must come back to smell cashews roasting.

Ma Shrireni starts the fire. A ribbon of smoke forms. It is the first in the Guinjata dunes and it smells like today. The sky is purple. Daylight is close.

She will make porridge for her family soon.

Ma Shrireni sits on her grass mat and watches her Mozambique, her Africa. The sun's face comes out of the earth. It is orange, full of fire. Ma Shrireni watches how quickly it makes a circle. The sky is pink.

From the hut, Lunga and her husband come. They are dressed. Her husband moves quickly. He says that they have no time to eat — Ma Shrireni and Lunga meet eyes. She tries to see inside him, read him like signs of the day's weather.

'*Ngiya-sharp* Mama.' He tells her he is fine.

Ma Shrireni wakes the girls and Tsitsu. They must say goodbye to their brother. Tomagashi and Mavis arrange their sarongs and doeks. The family collects around the fire but they will not eat together.

Her husband looks to Lunga, '*Mashambe*,' he says. Let's go.

Mavis's throat opens. A deep cry pours out. She runs to Lunga and throws herself at him, emitting raw weeps. The younger girls follow, circling him like the day's first coconut. Tsonga grips his left leg. Tsitsu stands close. Lunga looks only at his mother.

'*Izagke*.' Ma Shrireni's husband calls Lunga again. Come.

Ma Shrireni walks toward her son, carrying her Christmas tin. She places it at his side. He closes his arms around her. She closes her arms around him. They hold each other.

'God bless you, *hamba khale*,' she says. Go well. '*Hlala khale* Mama,' he says. Stay well. He lets go and turns toward his father.

The two men face the road out of Guinjata. The path to Johannesburg is familiar. A path taken before by this family.

Nkosiame.

Lunga.

Already, one son is lost to Mozambique. Another walks away. Maybe it is harder to watch him walk than to think of him under the waves. This is the same one, the same stone in her chest.

This is the story of the sun that stands up.

Ma Shrireni looks at the sky. It is thin and grey. Still not the colour of the sea. And empty of promise of change.

As she turns to the fire, a wail erupts from somewhere in Guinjata. The cry of a woman. It fills the space between the palm trees. It fills the dry air between the sand and the sky, flooding it with wet pain.

It comes from the stomach of Mozambique, from all the grief that has passed and all that is still to come.

These are the rules. The sun is hot.

The Cupboard

Lisa Schons

On that morning, the cupboard had turned red. When Anna entered the kitchen longing for a coffee, the thing glowered at her from its corner. She had been expecting something like it all along. The last days hadn't been easy. Once again the colour had drained out of the world, the coffee tasted bitter, she lost control over her thoughts. And now the cupboard had turned red. Still, this was new; the rules had been changed.

The cupboard had been there when she moved in; looming over the kitchen like an old tree with roots so deep they penetrated the earth's core. It was green and she liked it. She soon realised that it was alive, that the green was real green. Not the paint you splash on dead wood to add liveliness to your house, but green like life itself. It even dawned on her that the thing may be older than the house it was standing in, that the house had been built to fit around it. In her first inquisitive days she tried to move it to see what was underneath. She half expected the tiles to end on a square of damp, old earth, but as hard as she pushed, she couldn't move it an inch.

At first she liked it. Then came the days when she felt she was being watched, that she was not wanted. Uneasiness crept into her bones, her movements became self-conscious. She started dropping things, the cups shattering on the stone floor with a sound echoing too loud in the silent house, spilt coffee on a white tablecloth. Things got misplaced. Had she put the jar on that shelf? She remembered it standing on the counter just a day before.

She called the previous owner of the house, an elderly woman. She remembered the day she had seen the house for the first time, the half-timbered walls surrounded by trees, a river nearby, the excitement of the moment when the tiny, bent woman had opened the door. 'Like a fairytale,' she had thought; the perfect refuge.

Now Anna asked her about the cupboard — where had it come from, what was the story behind it? She tried a casual tone, faking a mild journalistic interest, but could not control the quiver in her voice. 'What cupboard?' the woman asked in earnest astonishment. 'You wanted the house to be unfurnished, and so I left nothing behind.' Confusion filled Anna's head. She barely heard the beep when the woman hung up. It had been here when she moved in, but had she seen it when she inspected the house? The images of that day became blurry in her head, started blending into each other like runny paint on a canvas.

And now it had turned red. Outside in the shed, Anna weighed the axe in her hand. She realised she was shaking. It had to happen this way, though she did not know what would become of her afterwards. But she had come here to forget and she would not tolerate this thing coming in her way, raising the dead. She gripped the handle harder and walked back in. The first blow felt intoxicating. She felt hard steel on soft, brittle wood, heard the crunching, saw the thing splintering, breaking. She only awoke from her frenzy when nothing but small wooden pieces littered the kitchen floor. Underneath she saw dusty tiles, no sign of earth or roots. Her cheeks flushed and she looked around as if expecting to find a silent, disapproving audience. Had she been overreacting? It was a piece of furniture after all.

Anna dropped the last sack into the bin on the street and without looking back she walked away. She cooked herself an exquisite meal that evening. She took her time, crushing the spices in her grandmother's stone mortar, picking fresh green herbs from the garden, and cutting the vegetables into identical little squares. She deeply inhaled the aromatic steam rising from the pots.

The next morning the cupboard was standing there, unchanged, immovable, and red.

Anna turned with a disgusted look, went outside and spent her day pulling out weeds in the garden. She couldn't stand the sight of the thing in her kitchen. Afterwards she threw all the plants she had ripped out onto a pile and set fire to it. Parched from the summer sun the weeds caught fire quickly and burnt with a low crackling until nothing was left. Incited by the flames, Anna took the lighter, walked into the kitchen and with trembling fingers held it to the cupboard. The fear of setting her house on fire flickered through her mind but she pushed it away. The ancient wood did not burn, but smouldered slowly away, leaving only a black smear on the wall behind it.

Anna leant against the opposite wall, watching the spectacle. When her legs grew tired, she slid down to the ground and sat there in the fading light, watching, waiting for the last glimmer to turn to ash.

She couldn't have said afterwards if she had fallen asleep or if reality changed in front of her eyes, but when the first rays of morning sunlight flooded the room, the cupboard was standing in its corner, unscathed, inevitable.

With a sigh she lifted herself off the floor, took a look around the room and shrugged. She walked over and opened one of the red doors. The hinges creaked in a perfectly studied, melodic way. She hesitated, lowered her head, a tiny, fragile silhouette in front of the massive furniture. Then, exhaling, she stepped in and closed the door behind her.

Silence.

Light changed into darkness, as day turned into night. The cupboard stood in its corner.

Noon the following day the red doors silently swung open and out stepped Anna, her clothing torn, covered in bruises, limping, but smiling. With endless tenderness she closed the red doors and placed her palms on the rugged wood. She could feel a weak pulse in unison with her heartbeat, getting weaker every moment until it stopped and from beneath her hands spread grey stone, consuming the cupboard's surface, leaving it fossilised, a dead monument.

Anna sighed, turned around and placed the kettle on the stove. She lit the fire and waited, with closed eyes, until steam rose from the boiling water. She drank the coffee, raising the cup to her mouth with steady hands, a serene smile on her face.

That night she carried the cupboard into her garden. Once so immovable, it now seemed to have no weight at all, a mere cocoon left behind after the creature is long gone. She dug a huge hole, tears mingling with the damp earth that soon stuck to her body. When all was finished she gave the grave one last satisfied look and turned her back on it.

In the following spring, little blue flowers covered the whole site, and after a while it became so overgrown, no one could have guessed what lay buried there.

The Terror (a Plea)

Tammy Wong

You smell of sour alcohol and cigarettes as you stagger towards me
Brash in the glory of false masculinity
In His image, but without His likeness*
Drunk and numb in your shame

I am your relief tonight, your soft relief
Soft against the hardness of your voice, your fists
That bottle in your hand
You are jealous; jealous and strong
Your abundant strength is my fear

The Terror.

Maybe you said sorry, maybe I said okay
I don't remember, but I know you lied
I lied too, but my body tells its own truth
You and me, we're making a shame-story together
And it's going to be a shame-baby we make

The terror comes again
The terror of you and your ways —

A cold stone set deep in my stomach
I can take it out
weigh it in my hand
worry it with my fingers
carry it in my pocket

Read Me

Wherever I go, the terror is there
It sharpens and dulls, but it never fades
The terror (of you) remains

I could teach our daughter to stand and walk
I could teach our son to walk and talk
But I need you
I can't show him how a man loves without fists
I can't show her how a woman loves without fear
We need you.

Please be strong for us

Be strong against the Terror

**Genesis 1:27; Colossians 3*

The Man in the Tree

Daniel Jenkins

> *How to write a short story: Put a man up a tree, throw rocks at him, get him down safely.*

One foot held tight in my outstretched hand, the other digging into my shoulder, I slowly manoeuvred the man to a position where he could grab hold of the branch. He hung there, swinging slightly in the breeze.

'Good. Now pull yourself up,' I said. The man, struggling, managed to heave himself over the branch and sat there with a blank expression.

'Now, climb up to the next branch.' He did.

'Now the next one.' He did.

'And the next.' He did, and in this manner I managed to get the man up a tree. I lit a cigarette and craned my neck to try to read his face. Still blank. Who was this man? He'd just been helped up a gumtree by a stranger, for no apparent reason, and all he did was sit there, not talking, not questioning, not giving me anything. His face barely visible, bark-coloured pants and a gumleaf shirt: it was as if the act of climbing the tree had made him a part of the tree, even the tree itself. And that didn't help me. I wouldn't have gone to all the effort of getting him up a tree if I'd known he'd just sit there and blend in. So I threw rocks at him. At first just little ones, more just pieces of congealed dirt. But these had no effect, so I went down my driveway to where the big rocks were. They just bounced off him. He was beginning to blend into the tree so much that my shots started missing. I found a few half-bricks behind the house and threw them. One got him right in the face, but he barely moved: not a sound, grimace or smile, not even an attempt to shield himself. Frustrated, tired and a bit confused, I left the man up the tree, went inside and cracked a beer.

It was Sunday morning and a baby elephant had just been born; a cricketer had split up with his fiancée; an entire state had flooded; another Indian bashed; a hail stone the size of a cricket ball; a celebrity overdose; a tradie killed by a pink bat; a 1986 Ford Falcon for sale; man seeks same, woman seeks man, Katherine seeks Marist Brothers class of 1968; house cleaning, tree lopping, births, deaths and marriages; Australia wins again. I closed the newspaper and looked out the window. He was still in the bloody tree. I could hardly see him but there was definitely a man-shaped dent in the leaves. I went outside and noticed my neighbour putting out her clothes. It was mainly underwear. Her blond hair fairly glistened in the morning sun. Her legs, tanned and tight, tiptoed over the dewy grass; her face craning skyward as her fingers delicately put each peg in its place.

'Morning John,' she said, feeling my gaze. 'How's the writing going?'

'Hey Shell. Lovely day. Yeah, the writing's alright, afraid I got bigger problems but.'

'Oh yeah? What's up?'

'He is,' I said, pointing to the top of the tree. 'I put him up there an hour ago. Having a bit of trouble getting him down.'

Shelley looked at the tree.

'I can't see anyone up there,' she said.

'He's there alright, he seems to have blended in a bit.'

Shelley looked harder. Squinted. As an artist, she had an eye for detail.

'Oh yeah, I think I see him. Gee, he really is the colour of bark and leaves. Maybe I could use him for a painting.'

'Maybe, he wasn't much use for me though. Kind of hard to work with.'

'Who is he?' Shelley asked.

'Dunno, just a man. He doesn't say much.'

'You tried throwing rocks at him?'

'Yep.'

'Nothing?'

'Not a word.'

'Wow. Let me go get my stuff.'

***

While Shelley went to grab her paints, canvas and easel, I went inside and filled the esky. If I was going to spend the day looking up a tree, I had to be well prepared. Also, this was the first time Shelley had crossed over into my yard, and the lonely single man in me wanted to make sure it wasn't the last. When I came back out Shelley was already set up. She sat perched on a wooden stool, brush in hand, peering up. I took a moment to study her. She was the kind of person who may have been ugly in high school. Too tall, a tad bird-like, she probably matured slowly, and had an awkward gait. Ignored by the boys, picked on by the girls, she withdrew into her own world — a world populated by fairies, imps, nymphs and waterfalls. Hitting puberty, she discovered an inner self that correlated with the impressions of Beauty she saw in the works of her favourite artists and writers — Ovid, Picasso, Shakespeare, Goya — and she cultivated an air of mystery which stayed with her long after her awkward gait disappeared. Now she was the one ignoring the boys. Long blond hair, a voluptuous frame, she spent more time in books and galleries than she did in backseats. Virginity intact, she chose underwear only for herself, but displayed them carefully on her line for only me to see …

***

'You got any beer in there?' She asked. Embarrassed, I snapped awake, sat down on the grass, and gave her a beer. For a while we sat in silence, drinking and looking up. Every minute or so she'd go to make a stroke of her brush then hesitate, sit back, ponder, sip, stare up, go to make a stroke, hesitate …

'It is strange,' she said finally. 'You can barely see him. I can paint the tree all right, no problem. And the sky, well, it's just blue. No problem there either. It's just that every time I think I've got him, he disappears, as if turned to leaves. Honestly, if I didn't know there was a man up there, I could swear we were looking at just another tree.'

'I know. It's my fault. I probably shouldn't have put him up there. Or at least done more research.'

'So you know nothing about him?' she asked.

'Nothing. I was inside, trying to make a start on a story, and the next thing I was helping this guy up a tree. I suppose I thought he'd do something, say something, at least try to get down.'

'Well, now that he's up there, we better do something with him. You've tried throwing rocks?'

'First thing I did.'

'Have you tried talking to him?'

For some reason that hadn't even occurred to me. I can help a strange man up a tree, but when it comes to polite conversation I've never been that good.

'No, I suppose it's worth a shot. You go first.'

Shelley put down her brush and stood up. She held her hands to her mouth and yelled:

'What's your name mate?' No reply.

'Where you from?' she tried. No reply.

'What do you do? What were you like in high school? Other than bark and gum leaves, what do you look like? Do you even like trees? Why are you up there? Why don't you come down?' Shelley yelled until her voice grew tired and still no reply.

***

'We're going to have to get him down,' she said, turning to me.

'I know, I know,' I said, cracking another beer and passing it to her. 'It just seems such a waste. I mean, here we are, me a struggling writer, you a talented artist, we have an esky full of beer and a man up a tree. Really, could it be any better? If only we knew what to do with him.'

'But we don't, we don't.' Shelley sat down next to me, her bare toes tapping on the grass. 'What if, now this is just an idea, what if you pretend to be him? I ask him questions and you answer for him. Then I'll paint him, sitting in the tree, the way you describe him?'

It was a good idea, I thought. With Shelley's direct line of questioning I quickly managed to get into character. I was up a tree, yes. Did I like it? It was okay. Of course I like trees, I wouldn't let myself be put up one otherwise. I didn't like having rocks thrown at me, no. Yes, it was a lovely day. But the questions soon became more personal. The beer and the heat, combined with my inadequacies in the field of character development, meant that my answers to her questions began to reflect not the imagined character of the man in the tree, but my own.

***

Yes, I was popular in high school. No, I never really liked art. I was a sporty kid: loved footy, tennis, running. I had a way with the girls, even lost my virginity to one in the back seat of my Falcon. It was awkward, yes, but it had a lot of power. Sold it for five hundred bucks to go to schoolies. Since then? Well, I've had a few jobs: dishwasher, bartender, fruit-picker, bricklayer — just to get me through uni. And now? Now nothing … I'm stuck up a tree. I have a masters degree, worked briefly in advertising, like long walks, sunsets, good wine … I like to travel widely but never well, I always end up sick or in jail. I like to read but not widely, I know what I like. Wife? No. Girlfriends? Some. I'm tall, tanned and twenty-nine, when I'm not up trees I'm at the pub or fishing.

***

'Alright, that's enough,' said Shelley, putting down her brush. 'I've got it, the man in the tree. I've got him. I think I've really got him!'

I looked up through the branches but couldn't see him any clearer, still just the vague outline of a man carved in leaves. Shelley gazed at the outline, her eyes catching the sunlight. She stood up and moved closer to the tree, all the while tilting her head to get a better look. Her singlet was dabbed with fresh paint and her uncovered thighs glistened with a greyish-green the colour of gum leaves. She stood statuesque, staring at the man in the tree.

'He's beautiful,' she said. 'If only he'd come down.' She slumped down on the grass next to me and I gave her another beer.

'You know, Shelley,' I started, thinking it was time I made a move, 'I'm really glad we're neighbours.'

'So am I, so am I.'

'I mean, there aren't many people who'd spend a Sunday with their neighbour staring up a tree.'

'I know, I know,' she said, still staring up the tree.

'I think we've a lot in common. You an artist, me a writer …'

'Quiet, John, I think he's about to say more.'

'I mean, I love Picasso, you love Picasso ...'

'Yes, yes,' she said, looking up through the branches expectantly. Her back was arched in such a way that her loose singlet began to fall from her shoulder, exposing the upper part of her left breast. With my right shoulder I nudged toward her, at the same time placing my hand on her thigh. I turned my head and softly spoke in her ear, 'I think the man in the tree has been quite auspicious for both of us.' Maybe not my best line, but one I knew had to be a prelude to a kiss. I moved my mouth toward her neck and kissed her behind the ear. No response. I kissed her again, this time letting my tongue linger softly on her earlobe. Again, no response. She just kept looking up the tree, her gaze fixed on the leaves. She looked like a Pygmalion statue, a frozen goddess. I moved my hand further up her thigh, my self-consciousness increasing with every inch of flesh attained. Warily, I tried to touch her cheek, which glowed like white marble, but was deflected by the flash of her hand. Shelley stood up. She dropped her VB to the ground and began walking to the tree. Flakes of white paint hovered in the air behind her.

'Shelley,' I called, 'what are you doing?' But I knew it was too late. I didn't even stand up as I watched my neighbour, a smile cracking across her face, grab hold of the lowest branch and pull herself up. She sat there, swinging in the breeze. She climbed the next branch, and then the next and, before long, she was nothing but a diaphanous shape carved in bark and gumleaves.

Shit, I thought, there goes another one.

***

I drank the last beer as the sun went down. I looked up. The leaves looked like schools of fish when seen from a boat: blurry sparkles waving back and forth, each one turning into the next with each change in current. The weather had turned. Storm clouds gathered near the airport, swallowing the planes as they came to land. I went inside and tried to write. Still nothing. I masturbated. I slept. I dreamed of Shelley, losing her virginity in the back of my Falcon. On Monday I woke up and looked out the window at the tree. He was still there. I couldn't see Shelley but I wasn't surprised. During the night I'd begun to wonder if I hadn't just imagined the thing with Shelley.

***

I went outside and picked up the beer cans, some still full, and threw them at the man in the tree. He still didn't move. Then I noticed the easel. It had fallen over in the wind and the canvas was wet. I picked it up, stood back, and looked at the painting. The overnight rain had made the paint run a bit, each colour blending into the other, but I could clearly make out the man in the tree. It was me. I threw the painting to the ground and ran inside. 'Put a man up a tree, throw stones at him, bring him down safely.' Fuck that, I thought, flipping through yesterday's newspaper. Man seeks same, woman seeks man, Katherine seeks Marist Brothers Class of 1968 … I kept flicking and finally came to what I was looking for. I picked up the phone. A man answered:

'Mat's Tree Lopping, Mat speaking.' Australia wins again.

Old Growth Forest

Petra Hanke

Darren, Boy Astronaut

Patrick Hsiao

Through the stars and over the moon.
All the things that make her swoon.
Just for her, he'll pull them down.
Then he'll be the talk of the town.

People will say, there he goes.
The little boy,
Who everyone knows.

In his fishbowl helmet,
He'll cross the sky.
For love, he'll tell them all,
For her, that's why.

He'll show her the planets that he'd seen.
All the stars, the galaxies,
And all the black holes in between.

She'll ask about his travels,
And the Martians he'd fought.
Then she'd say, you're my Darren,
Boy astronaut.

Amelia's Name Used to Start with a 'C'

Sonia Chan

Amelia's name used to start with a 'C'

When she was seventeen her cousin in Lebanon got engaged. It was not an arranged marriage; she was given a choice from a number of men that her parents had chosen for her. Amelia was not friends with her cousin, or in fact any members of her extended family. It wasn't that she didn't like them. It was just that they lived so far away and she had never met them.

But when Amelia was seventeen her cousin got married, in Lebanon. Her entire family was summoned: herself, her mother, father and three younger brothers. But none of them wanted to go — least of all her father. She had hoped that her eldest brother would have wanted to go to Lebanon because all he talked about was travelling. When Amelia had asked him he replied with something dismissive and didn't say anything more. Amelia sometimes wished that he had come along because then things might have turned out differently. But he didn't.

Amelia's name now starts with an 'A'. She is married, for the second time, and has three children. Her youngest is only seven months old, and the eldest child is ten. She never really thought her life would turn out this way. Amelia left her first husband. She married him almost immediately after returning from Lebanon just over ten years ago. He was a good man, but he was a labourer and liked to lie down a lot. When he would come home from work he sometimes forgot that she had been at work taking care of the children all day, and so in his forgetfulness he would lie down. Amelia had to cook him dinner while one child cried for her breast milk, and the other one ran around the house. He was a good man, but Amelia had to leave him.

Amelia wears a hijab now, but she didn't while she was growing up. It was only during her trip to Lebanon to attend her cousin's wedding that she realised she had an obligation to her religion, to her faith, to wear it. When she came back her mother picked her up from the airport, but she didn't say anything to her about her head dress. Her mother just dropped her at home and then returned to work. It was then that Amelia made a decision and a phone call.

The community was quite a nice environment. It was just a group of people with similar interests who spent time together, participating in activities. She knew that after the terrorism things of 2001 everyone was a little scared of the word 'Muslim' and 'Islam', but they were just a group of people who had fun. Amelia had fun with them. It was only a few months after joining the community that she made her request and was given three options. She chose the one with tired eyes and nice muscles. He was from Lebanon too, and he had a nice smile. He asked her to change her name.

They got married in a small ceremony with only his family in attendance; they were really strict, and they didn't have much money. His mother made her aware that she brought only a fertile womb to the family. It was on their wedding night that her first child was conceived. Amelia wasn't sad when she lay there on the stiff new sheets that still had creases from being folded in the packet. She wasn't happy either. But she liked her new name – Amelia – it made her feel feminine and different.

He was okay, the man with the tired eyes. Although Amelia soon learnt that he was always sleepy. He had to get up for work at 4am and he would work until dinner time, sometimes 7pm. Then he would come home and go to sleep. There was always money in their bank account and she was a simple girl who didn't need a lot of clothing or anything like that. But she wanted him to love her, passionately, like on TV shows and in the movies. She wanted him to come home, hot and sweaty from a hard day in the scorching sun, and envelop her in his arms, drowning her in his scent. She wanted him to feel towards her the way she thought she could feel towards him. But he never did. The same thing would happen every night; he would come home, kiss his daughters, and lie down and wait for dinner. Amelia would make it for him — she was very good at cooking — and she would watch him while he ate. His skin was dark from sun exposure, his muscles were hard, and the hair on his chest curled against his shirt and wreathed in and out of the gold chain that his mother had given him on their wedding day. After eating he would go to bed. Amelia would join him once the children were asleep and she would gently nudge him awake. They would honour their marriage and afterwards Amelia would take a little longer to fall back to sleep. He snored, and Amelia couldn't fall asleep if he was snoring.

Just once Amelia wished that he would take his shirt off. He never did. Just once she wished that she had dared to take it off for him. But, she never did.

When she divorced him she took the children. He didn't seem to care that much. He moved back to Lebanon and she never saw him again. She went back to her parent's house to find only her three brothers there. They were living together, alone under one roof. All of them single.

'Mum and Dad got a divorce. Dad lives with his new girlfriend, and Mum's in an apartment in Fitzroy,' her eldest, travelling brother said. Still seven years younger than her, he had become a man. He was skinny and he had long hair. He told her he was studying again. Her other two brothers were musicians. She stayed for a little while and let her brothers play with the children.

Amelia then spent three weeks at her mother's house until she married her second husband, a businessman. He seems better than the first. He holds her hand sometimes, and he doesn't have tired eyes. He likes her cooking and her children.

She still can't believe that this is the way her life turned out. But at least she has a family and someone to take care of her. When her children get older they can take care of her too. Amelia isn't like her mother. She has some sort of happiness, or security, or something. She has something. That's all that matters in the end.

Caroline gets a Brazilian and a full-leg wax

Caroline was born into a very confusing situation. Her mother is an Islander and her father is a full-blooded Chinese man. She grew up looking like neither of her parents, and only a little like her sister. Her dolls never looked anything like her, nor did any of the girls in the magazines or in the catalogues. As she grew up strangers began to think she looked Indian, especially when she burnt her wavy hair into straight lines. Those strangers would often approach her and ask her where she was from in India. She resented it when people did this. All those Victorian novels that she had to read for school had told her it was impertinent to speak to a stranger without first being introduced. Caroline grew up not knowing where she belonged and she grew to hate Indian people. This is unfortunate, because her father is a Chinese man who can speak fluent Hindi. Maybe she hates him a little too.

Caroline has never had a boyfriend. She is twenty-five years old and she has never been on a real date, except inadvertently. She thought he just wanted to have dinner, but it turned out that he wanted to have Dinner. It isn't that Caroline is incapable of Dinner, she just prefers to have dinner. Caroline loves food; sometimes more than anything else.

Another reason that Caroline never goes out for Dinner is because she is waiting. She is hoping that one man will come back into her life, even though he left her behind so many years ago with only a brief explanation.

Despite never having a real boyfriend, and also being a virgin, Caroline goes to her beautician once a month and gets a full-leg wax and a Brazilian. Every month she lies on the waxing bed, the paper underneath her crinkling with sterility, and Caroline wonders about her passionate celibacy. No one sees this part of her body, and in summer a bikini wax would suffice, but for some reason, like a narcissist, she always returns. Afterwards, usually a day or two later, the memories of pain having subsided, she walks around like a little girl with a secret flower in her pocket. She never lies to anyone and tells them that she has gotten used to the pain. It hurts a lot and sometimes she bleeds onto the crinkly paper and on her underwear.

Caroline is smart. She has an idea of how smart she is and of how many things she is capable of, but she doesn't want to guess in case she gets it wrong and finds herself bitterly disappointed. When she was in primary school she was too shy to answer questions or talk to her teachers, and so when she realised that getting good marks meant that teachers expected her to talk more, she purposefully tried to get bad marks. When Caroline began the first year of her PhD her mother asked her again what it was that she was studying. Caroline and her mother did not get along.

The greatest fear in Caroline's life is that she could be homeless any day. Caroline had a lot of free time in the evenings so she volunteered at homeless shelters and soup kitchens. She knew a lot of people who lived on the streets. People who were smart and talented, words that had been used to describe her at different points in her life. These people made one wrong decision, got addicted, and suddenly found themselves lying on the street, hoping a stranger would toss them some change. Caroline's second greatest fear is ending up in a loveless marriage. She wants romance, heat and passion. She doesn't want what her parents have. They are two people who were flying in the right direction, but who missed each other at a crucial moment. Now her parents are committed to this thing, bound by children and a mortgage. Also, Caroline is afraid of mortgages.

Caroline was born in Australia, but for as long as she remembers she has been watching television shows from America and reading novels from England. She always wanted to go away and travel to far and exotic places, change her name and become whoever she wanted to be. Maybe even to find a place where strange hybrids like her were not only welcomed, but celebrated. Although she never really articulated it in this way, she always just wanted to not be the only dark-skinned person in her group of friends. So when she was old enough Caroline travelled.

When she was in Spain, Caroline met a beautiful man, who smiled and laughed and talked about travelling. They were together all night — living their dreams and hiding from their fears. He was a hybrid, like Caroline. His mother was Lebanese and his father was Australian. The boy had soulful eyes, big and brown, and he had long curly hair. He was going to return to his studies when he went back to Australia. He was from Australia too. Caroline would never again remember a time when she felt so at ease, like she belonged.

Caroline wakes up early every morning and has a shower. She exfoliates religiously, all over her body. After her shower she makes herself a cup of coffee which she drinks while checking her email. She rides a bicycle to work at the university, and spends the first three hours of each day in silence, without talking to anyone. During those three hours she thinks of the beautiful travelling man she met in Spain and the dreams that she had about him the night before. After the three hours she switches him off and goes to the lectures and tutorials that make her money to live. When her work day is over she rides home in the dark, with one leg of her pants tucked into her socks and a reflector vest on her back. She makes herself dinner, but some nights she'll just eat yoghurt. She always goes to bed early because she wants to be in her dreams.

After a couple of years of communication with the man she met in Spain, Caroline heard from him no more. Caroline's pride would not let her pursue him. In her dreams they are married and they live in an apartment that they don't own. They hold each other, his body so close to hers that she feels his heat and he whispers her name — Caroline. In the morning they both go to work and in the night they return home to cook dinner for one another. Then they both go to bed early and lie awake, side by side. They don't need to dream of a better life.

Caroline gets a Brazilian and a full-leg wax just in case the beautiful travelling man returns. They'll have Dinner together. Caroline's fears will go away. She will buy a house, because she will feel like she belongs.

It's Meah, not Mia

When Meah was young her mother took her to a mothers' and babies' dance class. Before she was even old enough to walk Meah's mother would hold her up and dance around the room with her. Meah always suspected that her mother only did this because she wanted to make sure that all the other women saw her 'post-baby' body. Meah had been dancing ever since.

Meah didn't just dance, she loved dancing and she loved it for the same reason her mother did. She loved it because she was beautiful and she knew it and she wanted everyone else to know it. It was not conceited. It was just a thing that was true. When Meah danced she felt as if every eye that had ever lived was watching her. She felt the music merge with her body and she felt like she was the conqueror of all things. Meah loved to dance because when she danced she owned the world.

Meah's parents had lived on a farm. Her mother would walk with her to the train station and catch the train, and then the tram, into the city for her dance lessons. Her mother had decided that if she could not live the dazzling life that she had always wanted then her daughter would. Naturally Meah's mother was disappointed when Meah decided to go to university. She studied urban ecology, which caused her mother to cry for days. Her mother never forgave her. Meah's mother had decided long before Meah was born that she was going to be beautiful and that she would dance, and she would dance, and she would dance her way into the heart of a rich man, or something. Something like in the fairytales. Meah's mother had decided.

Meah turned twenty-one on the same day that a boy in her contemporary dance class turned twenty-two. He had been dancing almost as long as she had. He first arrived with his two brothers and his mother — a little woman with stern glasses and a hard jaw. Over the years his brothers stopped coming along, and eventually his mother didn't come anymore either. It was just him. He'd ride to class on an old bicycle that clanked and he'd be wearing worn out, faded track pants. He was skinny. Once Meah was partnered with him and she felt his ribcage through his skin as they moved together on the dance floor. She shuddered when she thought about it. They had known each other for five years before they spoke to each other for the first time. It was in the dizzying haze of puberty when Meah walked over to him and asked if he was gay. Gay, not homosexual. She didn't know that word then. He quietly said 'no', like a mouse, and continued stretching. The girls who had dared Meah to do it were giggling loudly as she turned and ran back to where they were.

Meah had been on an aeroplane once in her whole life. It was when her mother's sister in Tasmania died in a car accident, or something. Her mother had taken her and they had flown over the ocean and landed on that small island near the bottom of the world. Meah couldn't remember it. But her mother said that it was a beautiful day, she said it was a beautiful day for her beautiful sister. Now Meah only thinks about air travel in relation to funerals.

Meah had grown up to believe in a God, or someone. Her mother always read to her from a thick, old black book that had blood spilled on its pages. 'The red bits are the important bits', her mother would tell her. Meah didn't care. She only remembered one thing about being introduced to this God. One afternoon her mother read to her that the disciples changed their names when they were told to, and that their new name was their true name. Meah only remembered this because that afternoon at her dance class the skinny boy had called her Mia. 'Mia', he called her in front of everyone when the music had stopped. She turned to him and screamed: 'It's Meah, NOT Mia'. After years and years of knowing each other, he didn't even know her name.

Meah's father was the next person in her family to pass away. She didn't know him very well and so she could only cry for him with the detachment that one has for a sad song. Meah's mother didn't cry at all. This time Meah didn't have to get on an aeroplane to see the blackness of funeral clothes and coffins. It all happened on their farm — her father's home. The thick black book with spilled blood was pulled out and things were said and many people nodded in sympathy. Meah refused to accept anyone's sympathy. Because sympathy is the word you wrap around your own feelings of love. She felt guilty taking from the loves and feelings of others.

When Meah was old enough she married the quiet boy in her dance class. By the time they got married he had grown his hair long and had become well known in some academic circle or another, and had travelled the world. Meah didn't ask him too many questions. Their courtship had been one of tiredness and exhaustion. He was finishing an incomprehensibly studious project and she had been planning a show or two. Her certificate of urban ecology lay dusty underneath the sequins of her latest costume. It hadn't been very romantic, or anything like that. It had just happened. Somehow they came together and they just stayed that way. Meah wouldn't say that she's unhappy.

Some time later, when she's much older, Meah will turn back to that thick black book and think about what it really meant to her mother, if it meant anything at all. She'll wonder about what it means to her, Meah, and what it means for her husband. Her husband had been brought up with a similar book, but not the same one. Meah never had children because she didn't know what she could tell them if they were to ask her questions about the thick black book and its blood-stained pages. She and the skinny boy from the dance class spend the rest of their lives together. Meah dances, and then opens her own dance school. Her mother cries when this happens. Meah's husband works hard. He spends a lot of time travelling and earning money to support Meah's dancing.

On Meah's wedding day she didn't wear any sequins, and she didn't dance. She remembers her mother calling her by her new married name. As they stood side-by-side sipping champagne, her mother said, 'if only he was Australian'.

A Lament

Hae Min Kim

That part of you I could not bury,
I see always in reflection.
Your face so clearly stamped upon me,
I know I have your attention.
On days I'm drained of energy,
You're much easier to see.
Through that looking glass (my reflection),
I see you, though our eyes are different.
Painfully I wipe the tears,
Tracking your face (my own).
Thinking of your encompassing love,
Your peaceful face; the sad, sweet smile.
You dealt with me always lovingly,
Though I lashed you with my pain.
Sweet dearest one (so innocent) —
Forgive me for I'll ne'er forget.

Charming

Harriet McInerney

Do not go gentle into that good night ... *

Alec had disappeared the same day as Charming. This was significant, Maisie said. Laura didn't think so. Maisie also linked the sudden disappearances to the moth plague in the city that summer. Laura was again unsure of her sister's reasoning. Regardless, the walls of churches and alleyways were covered with a dense, rhythmic cloud of moths tumbling together to form a mighty unnameable beast.

It was in music classes that Alec and Laura had met, though they were both most passionate about art. When Alec said that Debussy reminded him of Monet, Laura understood. Together they sought to free themselves from the physical world and escape into the ethereal. The space of light and movement and sound. Laura was a landscapist, she watched the way clouds billowed and examined the ocean's wrath with her calm eyes. Alec preferred to draw faces. He drew distorted, frozen moments of fleeting expression. The kind of moment that lasts a millisecond. Microexpressions. Captured. He knew which muscles of the face were involuntary and liked to watch them in people. He also liked to imagine expressions, and he would title abstract drawings things like 'Mum when eating vegemite and tuna' or 'Father Joe's expression when finding a cockroach in his carrot and pea soup'. They were silly, quirky and boldly expressive. Looking at them made Laura feel alive.

***

Laura was very quiet when Maisie asked about Alec. No one knew where or why he had gone. His family were worried, but in their own free-spirited, bohemian way.

Maisie told Laura about Charming.

'His sudden disappearance, I suspect, was due to the moths.

Moths are a bother to everyone at night, but Charming particularly couldn't stand the fluttering of wings near his ears. You know, cats have heightened hearing and all.'

Maisie's voice rose and fell rapidly while she led Laura to the laundry, showing her the clues suggesting Charming's escape route. Laura was half listening. Mainly she was thinking about moths: their abstract beauty, the strange patterns they fly in, and the powdery, chalky dust you get on your fingers when you crush them. She recalled Alec, who at first had laughed at the moths, provoked them and wondered at their beauty. While walking home one day a stray moth had landed on his cheek making him giggle in delight. But as the moths grew thicker they bothered him more and more.

***

As it turned out, both Alec and Charming returned safely within a week.

When Laura spoke of Charming's similar disappearance, Alec wished he were a cat. No one would ask questions that way, they would just understand that he got scared or adventure-hungry or left to seek his fortunes in wider pastures. In fact, Laura and Maisie's mum told the girls that she had once read somewhere that cats are either attached to their home or their family. Perhaps Charming was a home cat, perhaps he was just searching for their old home, she had said.

***

Two weeks later Alec organised a night-time picnic. He brought asparagus sandwiches, a picnic rug, a kerosene lamp and homemade lemonade in an old two-litre coke bottle. Laura lay on her back and felt crushed by the sheer immensity of the sky, which folded out like a map before her eyes. The stars formed intricate patterns, held intimate relationships that she was incapable of comprehending.

'Look, the stars are spinning.'

She rolled over to see Alec, arms outstretched, spinning, as if preparing to take off into the night sky. The moths navigating their way towards the light flew up in shock at his vicious movement, but Alec spun so fast that they were scared to fly near him, should their delicate wings be hit by his propellers.

Eventually he became dizzy and toppled over, staggering into a tree trunk which eagerly scratched out in defence. He recoiled, fumbling his way through shrubbery to meet Laura back on the rug. They put out the light, but still the moths came, no longer drawn by the light but by the moth swarm. They were gathering numbers.

***

Maisie knew she needed to leave the laundry window open so Laura could slip in when she eventually came home. Maisie also knew that if she left the window open all night Charming would probably run away again, so crafty as always she fashioned a leash from her dad's skipping rope and gently tied Charming's collar to the chair he liked to sleep in. Contented, Maisie went to bed.

***

Laura heard him creeping away in the night. She doubled over with nausea, but she let him go. She knew he had to. He had to grab the moths in his clammy hands, one by one, feel their wings stop beating, and dust the chalk off his hands and clothes. Her tender protection could not save him. He wanted to go and she had to let him.

***

Just as the birds began to chatter Laura hitched her foot up on the terracotta pot and climbed in through the laundry window. As she swung her legs over the washing machine she noticed what she first thought to be a fur muff hanging precariously from the back of a chair. Then in a stream of realisation she knew it was Charming. His fur, ruffled in the breeze, gently caressed the back of the chair, his entire body flopped in a furred resignation. Maisie's neatly tied leash held sturdy, as unknowing of its role as noose as Maisie was of hangman.

A moth against the wall awoke and started flying towards the window, beating itself against the bleak glass. Charming could no longer respond in fear. He could no longer respond at all. While Alec raged on against the moths Charming was now powerless. It was the most melancholic thing she had ever seen.

'*... Rage, rage against the dying of the light.**

* From 'Do Not Go Gentle into That Good Night' by Dylan Thomas

BBQ Man

Rob Ashton

In Year Nine, I had hockey training every Tuesday after school. I didn't mind that my teammates never passed me the ball.

Our first training routine was to stand in two lines facing one another and pass the ball. Every boy, except me, shouted for it.

'Pass it to me, Greg!'

'Greg, pass it here!'

As Greg pushed the white ball firmly towards a teammate there was a half-moment's silence while hawk's eyes determined its destination. The call would rise up anew, 'John!' 'Here, John!'

My teammates were never mean to me. They silently knew that I was at the bottom of the social pole; they'd win no kudos by giving me the ball. Indeed, had they done so I would have felt embarrassed by the attention and guilty because they'd wasted a social opportunity.

***

That same year I realised I had to start mentally preparing for my twenty-first birthday party, a dreaded event that was seven years away. I was at a party (a rare occasion) feeling not too bad when the thought hit me, 'This party's okay but it's only small. And there are no cool kids. No way could I handle a big party, especially my own. I have to beat this fear before my twenty-first.'

Not having a twenty-first would have been humiliating. Somehow I'd have to make myself go to parties to gradually build up my confidence. I was determined to achieve my goal.

***

At eighteen I went to university for the first time. My uni offered a shyness course. One of the guys in the group said, 'I want to be able to ask a question in a lecture.'

His comment slapped me. His aim was impossible for me to imagine achieving — like running faster than Carl Lewis. My ambitions, though more modest, were still terrifying — and beyond me; like eating in the cafeteria and speaking in a tutorial. I withdrew from uni on the day of my first tutorial.

***

The next year I enrolled at teachers' college, determined to make a fresh start. At lunchtime I sat on the empty lawn. The cicadas' cries punctuated the heat while I ate dry sandwiches and stole looks through the windows of the cafeteria. Everyone seemed to be there. I wondered, 'How can they look so relaxed?'

Most of my week was an ordeal. From Monday morning until the end of my last class on Friday all I could think about was the weekend. I couldn't wait for a respite from stress, always pushing to the back of my mind the worst part of the whole week: Sunday night. I was doing my best to continue my studies but I couldn't take the relentless anxiety; my determination to make a fresh start lay in ruins. After four months I quit.

***

Around this time, still in the seven-year lead up to my twenty-first, I sought professional help. I felt like an emotional cripple. If only I could have gone to Accident and Emergency to get a plaster cast. But my problem was in the mind. I hated myself for not being able to beat it. Surely I controlled my own mind.

I briefly saw two psychologists before spending some weeks with a psychiatrist. I talked to Matt for fifty minutes every Wednesday while he wrote in his black file. I saw more of the brown curls on the top of his head than I did of his face. He told me I didn't need medication. That was all he said.

I was a patient, polite and timid nineteen-year-old, but eventually I had to ask, 'What do you have to say about my problems? What should I do?'

He raised his eyes from the file just long enough to say, 'What do you think you should do?'

I couldn't get him to say anything more. But I kept seeing him, until the day I mentioned that I'd left teachers' college and got a job. At the end of the session he looked up and prepared to say something. I was excited. Finally, I was going to get some direction. 'Since you're now working, you'll have to pay the full rate,' he said.

Hot blood pulsed behind my eyeballs. 'Is that all you can say?' I blurted out.

'I don't have to justify myself,' he said.

I paid his receptionist before leaving, never to return. As I stepped into the deserted street I thought, 'What now?'

***

I never did have a twenty-first party. My seven years of preparation had been a failure. I hadn't even gotten close to my goal. I felt like a loser.

When I was twenty-seven my friend Dean invited me to his younger brother's twenty-first. Somehow I forced myself to go. Except for the speeches I hated every second.

***

Later that year my friend, Anna, placed her Mona Lisa coffee cup on her white kitchen table, fixed me with aquamarine eyes framed by long lashes and said, 'Come to my twenty-first.'

A shot of dread hit my guts. I held Anna's gaze and concentrated on what I did best: inventing convincing excuses to avoid social situations. 'Keep looking at her,' I told myself. 'Looking away could make you look shifty. And you may need to lie.' (At times like this I realised, ironically, the drawbacks of having an empty social calendar.) A feeling of panic joined the dread as I pictured myself trying to arrive at her party. 'There's no way you can go,' I thought. 'Think of something quickly, before she gets suspicious.' I was terrified Anna would discover that I had social anxiety; my shameful secret.

At that moment Anna's eyes blinked closed and for the first time saying no seemed feasible. But a swish of eyelashes exposed hopeful eyes; I knew I wouldn't be making any excuses that day. 'I'll come,' I said.

Anna didn't know that she'd ignited a conflagration inside me. I sat opposite her trying to look calm while, at lightning speed, my mind repeatedly shouted, drowning out her French popular music, 'You have to go to a party you can't go to.'

The fire raged from that moment until the day of Anna's party weeks later. Her twenty-first was my first thought in the morning and last thought at night. 'How will I cope with the party? Is there any way to get out of it? No. I promised Anna. But how will I cope with the party?' And on it went.

On the night of the twenty-first I rang Anna but there was no answer. I rang again the next day. 'I'm really sorry I couldn't make it. I had a friend who was suicidal and I had to help him.'

My smooth lie meant I'd avoided both going to the party and Anna uncovering my secret.

'That's okay,' she said. 'I knew you'd have a good reason. Is your friend alright?'

***

I was twenty-seven when I met Anna, after enrolling in a Bachelor of Arts majoring in psychology; even though my main interest was politics. I chose psychology to learn how to beat my social anxiety. Nothing was more important.

I'd spent the previous year backpacking in South America. That experience gave me the confidence to think that I'd handle uni better this time. But my improvement was small. I still counted down the days to the end of every week, month, semester and year; all the while knowing that I was wishing the prime of my life away.

Somehow I finished my degree. But I never did discover the solution to my still-secret problem. A problem Anna never even knew I had.

***

Halfway through my degree I got a job in a government department. In one branch, we met every Tuesday morning around a grand polished oak table. The table's beauty was incongruous — juxtaposed as it was with the ugliness of my weekly misery.

Each meeting began with a briefing from the branch manager. Next, starting from his left and proceeding clockwise, we'd report on our week's activities. My palms would sweat. Much worse, my heart would pound. By the time my colleague two spaces to my right was speaking, my heart had extended from my chest into my throat, like an octopus extending thick grey tentacles upwards; tentacles that wrapped around my windpipe and squeezed.

I had no air ... I needed air to speak ... I had to speak. Twenty-five sets of eyes expected it. I couldn't say anything even when I had something useful to contribute. 'Nothing to report,' I sometimes said, pathetically.

I could say five syllables without inhaling.

***

In 2008 I heard about an experimental treatment of social anxiety at Sydney's Brain and Mind Research Institute. I rushed to make an appointment. Then I rang my mother.

'Have I always been like this?' I asked.

'Yes,' she said. 'You were always anxious around people you didn't know. You'd hide behind me and avoid looking at them. If you couldn't hide you'd fall asleep. The first time I took you to the barber you were eighteen months old. When you saw there was no way to avoid the situation you promptly fell asleep.'

I went to my appointment, and, several social anxiety questionnaires later, was classified as 'diagnostic'. My social anxiety was severe enough for me to be accepted into the course.

Each week, half of us took a low dose of a drug believed to assist learning; in this case learning how to use cognitive behaviour therapy to overcome social anxiety. The other half took a placebo. Neither we nor the therapist, Luke, knew who was taking what. I hoped I was on drugs — I wanted all the help I could get.

At the start of our first session Luke outlined what cognitive behaviour therapy was. The behavioural component meant exposing ourselves, mainly between sessions, to socially difficult tasks: 'exposure tasks'. Every week we'd have an exposure task to do as homework. Tasks we'd probably 'catastrophise' about. 'Yes,' I thought, as memories like my 'non-twenty-first' invaded my mind, 'that rings true.'

His next statement jolted me, 'The course runs for eight weeks for three hours a week. You may say that's a lot of time. But think of it this way. How many hours of your life have you felt socially anxious?'

It was a killer point. I looked around the circle of faces. Had the others been similarly affected? Everyone was listening intently. Something was happening in the room — the air felt thick. Suddenly I realised what it was: the powerful determination of people who'd suffered for too long deciding to fight. I felt a bond envelop us; we were in this together. It was as if Luke were an arms dealer offering each of us a Kalashnikov and a full magazine to kill our fear. In the twenty-four hours he'd have with us he'd show us how to disassemble, reassemble and clean our gun. But it was up to us to fire it.

Luke took our exposure task homework seriously. So did we. We started off with less difficult tasks (my first task was to go to a cafe) and gradually made them more challenging. Listening to the social agonies of the others had a big impact on me. I'd always known that my problems weren't unique but now, privileged to hear everyone's honest and raw stories, I saw many remarkable similarities between us. I began to wonder if my social anxiety wasn't as much my fault as I'd thought. But, though I didn't view the others as failures for not conquering their fears, I still felt like a failure for that very reason.

It was at the end of each session that we chose our exposure task homework. We chose the tasks ourselves — depending on what was most appropriate for us — with Luke's tactful guidance.

From the second session, the first thing we did each week was talk about how our exposure tasks had gone. In the beginning we were surprised. Where were these catastrophes we'd been expecting? Most of the time we'd had success. Even fun! (I'd ended up going to two cafes and chatting with the waitresses. Going to a cafe would never again be homework; it was too easy). Slowly we stopped assuming every social risk would end in disaster.

Luke was the only one who didn't seem surprised. But he kept quiet about it. He could have told us what we'd learn from the exposure tasks. But I guess he wanted to show us.

Late in the course, Svetlana made an announcement: 'I'm having a BBQ at my place on Saturday.' She flicked her fringe, spiked into blonde needles, out of her eyes. 'And I'd like to invite all of you to come.'

What shocking news! Was she mad? The irony was stunning. My

jaw dropped and my mouth stuck open stupidly like a children's cartoon character.

But I immediately accepted her invitation. Going to her BBQ was my homework for that week, tactful guidance not required.

This was my most challenging exposure task yet. It was a big deal. But the next couple of days were fine. That was huge progress compared to the lead-up to other social events. I began to hope. But the stress barged in seventy-two hours before the BBQ — the sort of stress that crammed my thoughts by day and made me fight my bedclothes by night. And it was at night that something horrible coursed through my body like a tide that allowed only fitful sleep. It made my heart bang against my ribcage and spread a sick feeling from the pit of my stomach to my Adam's apple. But unlike a normal tide it never went out.

I awoke exhausted on the morning of the BBQ. I lay in bed and stared at the white ceiling. Part of me hated Svetlana at that moment for putting me through this. But a bigger part of me recognised how much she'd helped me. Especially the time we agreed — before our session one day — that no longer were we going to be ashamed of our social anxiety. Our strong agreement gave me validation that I was right not to feel ashamed.

I disentangled my limbs from the damp bedclothes and sat on the edge of the bed. I didn't know how I was going to cope with the party. Even fully rested it would have been way too much. 'Just stay home,' I thought. 'It's the only way to get rid of this stress. No one can physically make me go.' I knew avoiding the party would immediately stop the unbearable stress. How I longed for that, even though I knew it would be replaced by about forty-eight hours of sickening guilt. 'Just stay home.'

But the image of Svetlana swam in my mind. I'd let so many friends down before, like Anna, and I was determined not to do the same to Svetlana.

So I was facing my familiar dilemma — I had to go to a party I couldn't go to. I closed my eyes and reminded myself of my exposure task successes; concrete evidence that I could succeed in social settings when I thought I couldn't.

I got up.

When the time came I marched to my front door and flung it open. Finally, I was achieving a goal. I stepped out with my Kalashnikov. It was time to fight.

But a funny thing happened on the way to the train station. I started to feel calm. I began to think of the BBQ not as a battle to be won, or at least survived, but as something to be enjoyed. That was a revolutionary thought.

I'd always visualised my social anxiety as a cliché: a thundercloud. But I wondered if a Kalashnikov would be effective against such a billowing substance. Maybe there was a better way: what if I could relax?

***

From the street, I could smell the smoke wafting up from Svetlana's backyard. I double-checked the number on the unit's door; after all this build-up I didn't want to walk into the wrong BBQ. 'Yes, this is it.'

I approached her garage. It was here, she'd told me, that she was sometimes trapped in her car by cockroaches that wouldn't move from the driveway or from the side of the garage door. 'Just get out and shoo them off,' I said.

'No,' she said, horrified. 'When I try, they run straight at me!'

I started to think that this was one of the stupidest things I'd ever heard. But I stopped.

'Hypocrite,' I said to myself.

'That must be a real problem,' I said.

'It is. Sometimes I have to ring Diego and ask him to hurry home. Luckily he doesn't mind. But once I was trapped for forty-five minutes.'

Around the corner of the garage was Svetlana's open backyard. The wide wooden gate was open. I saw Svetlana sitting opposite. She spotted me, sprang up and rushed over. 'I'm so glad you're here,' she said, reaching up to kiss me.

She introduced me to her flatmate, Diego, who was standing beside us. He was in charge of the sizzling meat I'd already smelt. 'We've got beef, lamb, pork and chicken,' he volunteered, his brown Argentinean eyes sparkling through the smoke.

'Come on inside,' said Svetlana, flicking her fringe out of her eyes. 'I want to show you around.' She showed off her spotless and perfect unit with obvious pride. I thought of saying that this seemed to be one aspect of her life that she could strictly control. But I kept quiet.

We finished the tour in the kitchen. She introduced me to her boyfriend, Ben, who'd just walked in.

Suddenly I felt foolish standing there holding my drinks. 'What should I do with them?' I worried. 'Put them in the fridge? Or is there a tub with ice in it? Am I supposed to know?' I'd been to so few BBQs in my life I didn't know how to behave. I felt my confidence fading. I was in a BBQ catch twenty-two.

'Would you like to put your drinks in an esky?' Ben said.

Esky! Great, I thought. I can do that! But where are the eskies? Panic started. I had to get rid of these drinks fast. I silently implored Ben to take them but he didn't.

'Oh yeah,' I said, oh so casual, as if what to do with my drinks was the furthest thing from my mind.

He led me outside to a line-up of eskies and removed one of the lids revealing deep rocks of ice. Gloom rose inside me as I realised I had to decide whether to remove the thin cardboard holding the stubbies together. Even worse, the eskies were beside the two trestle tables filled with the party people I hadn't yet met. I felt like I was on a stage. I could feel them watching me thinking, 'He doesn't know what he's doing. Anyone would think he'd never been to a BBQ before. At his age he should know how to behave. What a loser.'

'I've handled machete-wielding bandits, gangs of thieves, and corrupt policemen and immigration officials in Latin America,' I thought, 'yet I can't put drinks in an esky.'

I felt on the cusp of a catastrophe, what a joke to think I could handle a BBQ. I'd had eight weeks of cognitive behaviour therapy. And I expected that to overcome forty-three years of avoidance? I'd fled parties before. And right then I knew I had to escape.

But I held on, even though in my panic I'd forgotten everything Luke had taught us. Or had I? Somewhere in my mind homework successes were swirling. They gave me a moment's clear thought: 'I'll just chuck these in the esky, cardboard and all. No one cares what I do. I'm not the centre of the universe.'

I plunged them into the thick ice, while simultaneously extracting one of the stubbies from its cardboard surroundings and retaining it in my hand, surprisingly deftly. I proceeded to unscrew the cap to open it (having been assured by the bottle shop salesman that they were screw tops) thus avoiding any possibility of a loud and excruciating search for a bottle opener.

I almost bumped into Svetlana as I did so. She must have followed me. She led me to an empty chair and, amid a flurry of fringe flicks, introduced me to the trestle table people.

I'd read a newspaper article days earlier saying that people loved being asked questions. So I asked the woman sitting opposite me a question. As I did so I realised that the thundercloud had gone. I talked to more people. I felt relaxed. For the first time in my life I was having fun at a BBQ.

Just as I finished this thought, a delighted cry went up from two of the women on the nearby table. 'Liz, Liz,' they called, evidently at the little girl entering the backyard in between her mother and father. I learnt later that they were Svetlana's neighbours.

I was struck by the man's saunter. He couldn't have looked more relaxed.

I imagined the next-door scene minutes earlier, the man dressed in a loose T-shirt and shorts, sitting in his armchair watching the NRL.

'Darl' we really should head over to Svetlana's,' I heard his wife say.

'Oh, do we have to babe? I'd rather stay in and watch the game.'

'Come on. I said we would. Besides, it'll be fun for Liz.'

Uncomplainingly — I sensed he was a wise man — he rose and slipped on a pair of thongs. 'I'm ready,' he said.

How different, I thought, was his build-up to the BBQ compared to my seventy-two hours of stress.

All these thoughts raced through my mind in the time it took the man to take only two or three, admittedly slow, steps. I realised that he wasn't telling me how to relax. He was showing me.

And he wasn't even trying to show me. Come to think of it, perhaps that was the point.

As I watched him, my mind swept back a generation; back to the lawn beside the teachers' college cafeteria. I felt the urge to stand up, enter the cafeteria for the first time and join my classmates.

I returned to my previous engrossing conversation. When I looked up the man was gone. I've thought of him scores of times since. I can channel his feeling of relaxation. I think, if he can do it, so can I.

He came along at the right time. Luke and Svetlana had set the stage and he'd sauntered in on cue.

Before starting Luke's course the anxiety level I'd have felt at a party or BBQ, when measured on the one to eight scale we used, would have been a definite eight. After Svetlana's BBQ it dropped to about two or three.

I've been to parties and BBQs since that day and enjoyed them; building up a stock of positive experiences to draw upon to boost my confidence. But it's always the man in Svetlana's backyard I think of when anxiety strikes.

I'm glad he gave up his NRL game that Saturday. To this day I still don't know his name. I call him BBQ Man.

(All names changed — including Svetlana's, even though she was happy for her real name to be used)

Good Dirt

Louise Carey White

You know you're at home when the dirt is good.

The best dirt is red, like an evening sky
yellow, like the sun
and black, like we are.

Good dirt has to feel a certain way.
It is cool, moist,
and cradles your bare foot
as you sink a little way in.

Good dirt attaches you somewhere.
With a watery whisper, your footprint is there
sealing your soul in the gentle, ochre earth,
bringing you home to your people,
your stories,
your place.

You can't sink your feet into concrete.
Concrete is whitish and doesn't cradle your foot.
It smothers the good dirt.
No more people.
No more stories.
No more place.

My people value the land, as yours do,
but you will never hear my people say do-I-hear-two-million.
No.

The value is how far into the good dirt
your bare foot sinks.

A trip away from the city is purifying
like good clean smoke.
That's where there's good crisp air and good green grass,
and after the yellow sun pours itself out of the red sky
there's real country darkness —
good dark black.

The wise women of my people always told me
that a good life needs people,
stories,
and place.

You know you're at home, they told me,
when the people,
stories,
and place
are grounded firmly in good dirt.
Real good dirt.

On the Wind

Ashley Kalagian Blunt

She was assigned the task of capturing the wind. This was something that had never been done before, but the times called for it. The wind had always proved troublesome. It ruined otherwise warm, cheerful summer days with its incessant blowing and howling, brought cold fronts and winter storms, spread fires wildly, tormented defenceless tropical islands. How such a brazen creature had been permitted to roam the planet for so long could only be explained by its incomparable size, its stealthy nature, its unceasing determination.

And she, serious and quiet and thoughtful, maybe unique but maybe not, she was charged with the task, not so much for these qualities, and not so much even because it was the general belief that she would succeed — though it was — but because it was known officially in the organisation that she was terrified of failure. This key piece of information had been typed into her file and italicised to bring it immediately to the reader's attention. It swung the decision in her favour (so to speak), because it was commonly known that someone afraid of failure would try tremendous, desperate things that others couldn't dredge up from their deepest dreams.

That day, she stood in the midst of the widest, most open field and stared down the wind. Did it suspect her, she wondered? Could it know what she had to do? She could not turn down the assignment; such a move would be the death of her career. No, she had been assigned to capture the wind, and she would. But how? How could she possibly contain something that was everywhere at once, covering the whole earth, constantly moving, something so powerful it swayed buildings of steel, something so angry it twisted itself into dizzying fits, throwing homes up into the air with cavalier fury?

In the midst of the widest, most open field, the wind rushed past her, not noticing her, as it had never noticed her before. She was not a scientist; she knew nothing about the wind. Could it be confined? Trapped in the desert and left to amuse itself blowing sand about for all its remaining years? After all, whom could it bother there? Some sunburnt creatures, perhaps; nothing there was profit in. But how to contrive to keep it there? The wind could not be bought, coaxed or cajoled. It acted like a small, tireless child amuck in a toy store. There seemed nothing that could convince it to desist its behaviour, no bribe it might accept.

Perhaps it could be processed for mass-market consumption. Kept in cold storage and sold off for private use in pre-sized boxes. Or were its only applications industrial? What kind of distribution network would be required? Trains might be reasonably sufficient, she calculated. Her superiors would find this situation ideal, she knew, but it seemed too complex and difficult — too risky.

She spent three days in the field, the wind shifting direction around her, tangling her hair in her face and threatening to escape with her scarf. Three days was as much time as she could afford before the nascent fear that her progress would be judged negatively began ice-picking its way along the tendrils of her nervous system. Could the wind be encapsulated in some sort of container, and left to roam freely but identifiably, high up in the sky? Perhaps in a well-labelled canister with bright yellow caution stickers affixed to it? One would look up, see it softly drifting overhead and say, 'Oh look, here comes the wind.' Idle heads would glance up, and a mother would point to draw the gaze of a young child who, of course, had never experienced those days when the wind had been permitted to dash about unfettered. Captured thusly, it might drift into the buildings that were climbing ever higher into the sky. Could it harm them? No. It would be light enough to be dislodged with the push of a hand. Perhaps the containing material should be transparent, to prevent complaints of its transit blocking the sun. We all have enough clouds in our lives, she thought.

At dusk on the third day, she settled on her answer. She would entrap the wind — contain it in clear, spherically shaped packaging and leave it up in the infinite space of the sky. There was less profit to be made, perhaps, but profit had not been her main objective, as was clearly outlined in her assignment.

The logistics proved difficult. It took several weeks to find suitable material, have it tested and tweaked and prepared properly. During this time, she lived on pins and needles, trying to show progress where there was no progress, inventing figures and facts for charts and graphs to indicate future successes of which there were no guarantees. She felt the awkward moistness of unwanted eyeballs on her at all times.

She took charge of the designs, the testing and retesting, the simulations rigged up in huge airfield hangars, the rented-by-the-hour cinematic wind machines set on 'cyclone' ripping at the sheer, expandable plastic film that was spun like silk from vats of thick, noxious sludge. Doubt festered at every step, every decision. What if something collided with it, punctured it? Repairs would be needed, mid-air, before the wind escaped and a costly project to recapture it had to be mounted. What if, due to heat waves and sunrays and the shifting seasons, the wind expanded beyond the limits of its prison, causing the whole thing to burst and litter some innocent area with toxic plastic debris?

More questions led to more experimenting, which led to more reports, and the reports piled up faster than anyone could read them. Filled with probabilities and statistics and pie charts, they waited indifferently to impart their recorded findings. Her budget evaporated into testing, making deadlines irrelevant. If she didn't push forward, there would be no money to complete the project. Decisions were made, supplies were ordered, progress marched on.

Again, she stood in the field and the wind blew, but everything was transformed. She was surrounded now not just by the wind, but by equipment, contraptions, mechanisms, by trucks upon trucks with hoses and hook-ups, by subordinates with clipboards and lab coats and helmets. She took charge of every piece, every person, every detail. Technicians scrambled amongst the equipment, the wires coiled in messy piles, the sky hung grey, the wind whipped up and around, past everyone and everything. Convoluted metal erections climbed from the trucks into the sky — into the path of the wind.

Gradually, quietly, exactly as projected, an ever-expanding bubble of sleek, slippery synthetic glory stretched up above the scurrying staff, above the trucks, above the contrivances straining to control it.

The wind pushing its boundaries further and further, the film of plastic shuddering against the pressure. It took three days, a warped reflection of the three days she spent thinking, planning. She didn't eat or rest or blink her eyes. This may have caused her misstep. No one saw it. The equipment needed monitoring, the mechanisms needed maintenance, the whole thing was winding up. Everything was exhausted, including the wind. Did it know it was trapped, recognise its situation? Could it feel the barriers surrounding it, its greatly reduced space? If so, or if not, no one cared, no one looked. As determined in the planning meetings, the procedural discussions, the final stages of the flow charts, they sealed it off, they cut it loose. It drifted upwards, slowly, with nothing to push it in any direction. They shut down, packed up, drove off, leaving muddy tracks and nothing else in the field.

Did they notice her absence? No one reported it. When she didn't show up for work, it surprised them. She had succeeded so succinctly: within budget, on time, without complaint. They waited patiently, and then impatiently, and finally they wrote her off. It was a disappointment; this success would have meant good things for her.

It had been one step too far. Something needed checking, though what it was she hardly remembered — perhaps the structure of the apparatus right at the very point where the wind went from eons of freedom to its future of aimless imprisonment. One moment she was standing, reaching, bending, her foot lifting to adjust itself backward just a step, half a step, not much, when her balance vanished, her whole body shifted, the air disappeared from her lungs. She was tossed up in the air, spiralling, her path convoluted, erratic, too fast to interpret.

How much time passed before she could breathe again? She was up, far up, tumbling, spinning, panicked. She couldn't think past this panic, couldn't work out her options. Her mind tumbled as rapidly as her body. Her hands reached out desperately for something to grasp, to hold onto, to stop her, to hold her down, but they encountered nothing except the occasional brush of uncaring plastic.

Her eyes searched, hunting for anything, but she saw only mangled stretches of grey, blue, white, speckled black and a sporadic splash of greenish brown. She was moving fast, it seemed, very fast, but she had no perspective, nothing for comparison. She felt sick. Did the wind recognise her presence, or would it have torn itself about inside its permanent penitentiary just as wildly without her?

She tortured herself in desperation, at first. Escape, escape! But in mid-air, this was impossible. She knew the details, the numbers. This noxious, chemical substance, the height of technological manipulation — she couldn't puncture it. They'd have to retrieve her, she realised in anxious terror. The costs it might incur, the effects on her career — on what should have been such a success! And the way people would look at her, those amused, mocking glances: the agony of it overwhelmed her.

Weeks passed. She wasn't aware of them. The wind calmed, losing its energy, or, at least the will to beat itself against the smooth slickness of its enclosure. She came to rest on the bottom of her shared prison vessel, her body supine, she supposed, the wind ruffling her hair and clothes without zeal. Her eyes stared vacantly at the haze below. She was too high up to distinguish any features of the land, and for much of the time she drifted over steely blue expanses of disheartening water, filled with desolation and loneliness. Not knowing where she was, not knowing when it was — she had never experienced this. The muscles in her neck, her face, her hands, unclenched. Her mind cleared.

Months passed. She realised, with an unfamiliar calmness, that her elevation was far too extreme. She would never collide gently with even the tallest office tower, see the shock of recognition and confusion on some executive's face as she floated closer and closer toward the protective glass separating them. In more time, this ceased to matter. She breathed more slowly, wasn't always nervously glancing over her shoulder, worrying about something unnoticed, forgotten, innocently incorrect. There was nothing but the caress of the wind and the tautness of the plastic film, the warmth of the sun and the chill of the moon. When she appreciated this, she failed to distinguish between the land and the water below.

Just as she didn't notice the time passing, she didn't notice her enclosure's parameters changing around her. How many years passed before the wind failed to fill the miles of space allotted to it? A keen observer (hypothetically, of course, as none existed: for those below, the wind survived only as an irritant of an antiquated past) would have noticed over time that the gently drifting capsule seemed to be condensing in on itself. Was the wind dissipating, evaporating, escaping? But no concerns bubbled in the mind of the container's accidental occupant, nor did she feel any sense of identity beyond the space that she shared with the wind. The space was shrinking so slowly she was unaware of it. She imagined the wind longing for endless plains, weather-beaten mountaintops, plunging valleys. She imagined it free, relieved. She couldn't ask it. If it had a language, she hadn't learnt it. And now it was fading, receding, contracting, her home and existence together with it, coming in closer all around her on all sides. And still she didn't notice, didn't move, supine but now with her face to the stars and her eyes closed, seeing nothing, sensing nothing, yet still alive and thankful for the reprieve, thankful that the fears and worries and anxieties that had weighed her down her entire life were gone, bound to the earth by their own heavy gravity. And this was what she felt even as the bubble of tired, weathered plastic shrank in all around her, the wind no longer there, and perhaps no longer anywhere, perhaps exterminated, and in that state she rose further and further away from the self she had left behind until there was no self at all, only the feeling of relief and gratitude and nothingness.

Lost

Dinnah Gustavo

Ladykiller

Isabel Robinson

There's nothing staid about me.
Legs splayed in a beach chair,
my bald gut bared
to match my hair.

A tongue of rock
licks the sky.
Grim, ancient,
its face wrinkles
under our feet.
A view to die for.

Our tent clasped in prayer
on the mat of tangled grass.
The leaves of green canvas
folded round the poles
like drunks leaning into walls.

Ground thick with wet leaves,
a brown carpet on a black floor.
She sees my eyes, the pupils
narrow as a closing door.
A moth flutters in her throat.

My hard hands hot on her back,
a fan across her shoulders.
She stands on air
then falls,

pinned by branches
to a spear of bush.

No one but me can hear that cry.
Mammon gives me breath and strength.
The tight zeros on a ledger's line
the six-figure sum,
the badge I pin my hopes to.

Sarge

Louise Carey White

Goddammit, I do hate that goddamn sound.
More tea, son? Good for the nerves.

Stop that shaking, you're almost as bad as those bloody guns.

You're a little quiet today …

Something wrong? Are you listening to me?

As I was saying, those German bitches will be off their schnitzel by tomorrow.

Auf Wiedersehen, Arschloch!

You're looking a little pale, boy.

Something wrong? Are you listening to me?

You Paved My Path, Why?

Ebru Okan

You laugh as corruption laces
The corner of your smug eyes,
Laugh as my emotion braces
The storms brewed from your every stride.

Taunted with no man's blessing,
I ask the horizon why,
The stars sent men pacing
Through my land, oceans wide.

With injustice comes many lessons,
I know this is the reason why
Silent streets lie empty facing
Shortages cathedrals high.

You look and judge, forgetting
You know the reason why
Our generations
came descending,
In tides
centuries wise.

An adoptive man's dressing,
All innocent in disguise,
Forgot that it's no man's professing
How future lives should strive.

Next time you come envisioning
How future paths should fly,
Don't forget the lost roads giving
Your events lullabies.

For if one tells you,
'This is it, say goodbye,'
You shouldn't lie reminiscing
On actions you cast blind eyed.

You Paved my Path, Why?

Contributors' Bios

Rob Ashton

Rob Ashton wrote his first story in Costa Rica. Thankfully it never saw the light of day. Since then his writing has appeared in eight publications including *Honi Soit*, *The Bull*, *Hermes* and *The Sydney Globalist*. He's proud that his personal story — 'BBQ Man' — is part of *Read Me*.

Thomas Azzopardi

Thomas Azzopardi studies Arts. Getting published has always been a crazy dream of his, which he now excitedly finds realised. Still experimenting with different styles and genres, his writing varies from comic parodies and poems to more philosophically minded pieces. He draws his inspiration largely from his friends and studies.

Sarah Bendall

Sarah Bendall has always had an overactive imagination and, aged six, wrote her first story about a ghost, a girl and her cat. Gothic horror, history and the fantastic inspire her writing. She is currently working on numerous short stories as well as a novella. This is her first publication.

Jacqueline Buswell

Jacqueline Buswell has just completed her Master of Arts in Creative Writing. She writes prose and poetry, translates from Spanish and studies Italian.

Louise Carey White

Louise is an undergraduate. Her interest in writing goes back a long way: school reports read, 'Poor maths skills. Cannot concentrate. Writing very well developed'. During her gap year, Louise travelled around Europe to further her interests in history, politics and culture: she aims to communicate these interests through poetry.

Annabel Carr

Annabel completed a BA (Hons) in 2005. She is currently a tutor, lecturer and PhD candidate in the Department of Studies in Religion. Her thesis examines the recurring image of the Lost Child in Australian folklore, and she has a long-standing interest in photography, both analogue and digital.

Laura Chan

As a science student, Laura is moved by the intricate beauty of living systems. Writing allows her to express this awe. The Chinese cabbage *Brassica pekinensis* is her favourite vegetable.

Sonia Chan

As a child Sonia used to make all the gift cards and letter writing paper for her family. Now she knits them items for the winter. Love is in our hands as much as it is in our hearts. Sonia hand-writes her stories.

Alison Gibson

Alison is a former philosophy student, current temp worker and video store clerk, who loves how short stories can show tiny glimpses of interesting lives.

Dinnah Gustavo

Dinnah is a Bethel University student from St Paul, Minnesota US and she hopes to be a special education teacher one day. She loves creating in every form: cooking, baking, painting, photographing and much more. She loves seeing God through every form of creation! This world is full of beauty and she believes that she is a part of this creation.

Petra Hanke

Petra Hanke is a Master of Applied Science student with a passion for wildlife and nature photography. She has travelled Australia extensively. In Tasmania, she was captivated by the old-growth forests she visited, and impressed by the stamina of local interest groups, fighting for their preservation as important wildlife habitat.

Patrick Hsiao

Patrick's parents were big storytellers when he was little. It's been written in ink for him since then.

Daniel Jenkins

Daniel is a writer slash bottleshop attendant living in Sydney. In 2007 he was shortlisted for the Queensland Young Writer of the Year Award. He is currently working on a novel while finishing his Master's. Writing 'The Man in the Tree' was a distraction from these two things.

Ashley Kalagian Blunt

Ashley is a Master of Cultural Studies student from Canada. Her short stories have won several prizes including the Carol Shields Creative Writing Award, and she has received a creative arts grant. She has previously lived and worked in Korea, Peru and Mexico.

Hae Min Kim

Hae Min Kim is a student at the University of Sydney.

Harriet McInerney

Harriet McInerney likes to write on public transport. Lately, she has been constructing a tale about very small women who live in fruit bowls, undetected because their dresses look like pears. If her psychology degree and amateur prose don't work out, she would like to be a full-time birdwatcher.

Ebru Okan

Completing a Bachelor of Economics, Ebru achieves her ambitions despite the odds. During her major in philosophy she became certain of her pursuit of humanitarian principles. There is no reason for writing other than expressing the emotions and thoughts that are enclosed in the iron cage of one's heart.

Isabel Robinson

Isabel is working on a crime novel set in Victorian London for her Master of Creative Writing. She also loves books and films, from which she steals ideas without shame. She lives with two cats and her family somewhere in the Inner West.

Marija Rodriguez

Marija grew up in a delicatessen, with a multi-ethnic family, where pickling cabbage and knife throwing were taught at an early age. She currently lives in Sydney with her husband, el carnicero, her mastiff, and a one-eyed cat.

Lisa Schons

Lisa is a writer/editor from Germany, the land of the Brothers Grimm. Her children's books and short stories are influenced by motifs from childhood fairytales as well as magical realism. Her passion for travelling is another source of inspiration. She is currently finishing her Master's.

Harriet Westcott

Harriet has a passion for writing and has penned fiction aimed at both adult and young readers. She is currently studying sociology.

Tammy Wong

Tammy is a law student with an interest in Indigenous legal issues. She enjoys writing poetry as a hobby and is still thinking of ways to combine these two passions. She feels most inspired to write when confronted with the heartbreak, courage and vision of the First Peoples of Australia.

Connie Ye

Woman-child. Happy to be published.

Michela Ziady

'Stone in Her Chest' is a simple story that we all know — one of loss — told in a way anyone can access: simply. It's a project of storytelling. A project of language. Michela completed the Master of Creative Writing this year and now works as a copywriter.

Editors' Bios

Louisa Althans

Louisa Althans is currently completing a Master of Publishing, has a business administration and marketing background, and enjoys literature and sewing. A native of Germany, she has previously lived and worked in the UK, the US and Namibia.

Tori Brownrigg

Tori Brownrigg is an avid reader, writer and traveller. She has recently completed her Master of Strategic Public Relations and is currently working in advertising at McDowall Creative.

Lex Hirst

Lex Hirst loves language in all its forms. A French and Spanish major with a Master in Publishing, she delights in being surrounded by eccentricity and colour. Her idea of paradise is lying in a hammock on a tropical beach with a great book and mariachi band playing in the background.

Patrick Hsiao

Writer, editor. Interests include sport, science, art and literature. Patrick is also fascinated by writing implements, pens, paper and he is hunting down a typewriter. So far it's been a crafty bugger.

Nadia Junaideen

Nadia Junaideen is a Master of Publishing student with a BA in English and History. She is a visual thinker, a frequent tea-drinker, a rhymer, a reader, a neighbour's-cat-feeder, a part-time designer, a sentence refiner, a compulsive multitasker and a truly terrible cook.

Lindsay Liu

Lindsay Liu loves books. Though she doesn't have an English background, she had great fun reading and editing English stories. She hopes that one day Australian books will be available in the Chinese market.

Pippa Lyons

Pippa's background is in interior architecture but she realised she might be in the wrong field when she was spending more time editing proposals than designing. She now coordinates international buy-ins at Murdoch Books and dabbles in web editing at Alfalfa House.

Olivia Porter

A word enthusiast and lover of all things literary, Olivia first realised that she had a knack for publishing when she found herself editing numerous papers for family and friends. She has moonlighted as an editorial assistant at Open Forum, and Simon and Schuster while completing her Master of Publishing.

Kristen Rooke

Kristen Rooke is a Master of Publishing student and also holds a combined Arts/Law degree. Her background is in legal publishing, but she enjoys editing both fiction and non-fiction. She works as a legal editor with LexisNexis Australia.

Lisa Schons

Lisa Schons is a publishing student. Originally from Germany, she has worked as a freelance journalist and editor in different countries and enjoys getting to know new cultures and languages. Lisa also writes children's books and short stories, one of which is included in *Read Me*.

Kelly Stock

Kelly Stock is a writer and editor finishing her Master of Publishing. Fascinated by the intersections and transitions between cultures, she enjoys writing about travel, literature, fashion and art. Kelly is establishing a career somewhere between her native Australia and adopted home in Canada.

Veronica Tang

Veronica has an innate fondness for the scent of ink on pages. She doesn't embrace much creativity but she loves the sense of completion. Missing a full stop at the end of a sentence is disastrous. She believes that reading is an exploration journey to find oneself. Books never die!

Acknowledgments

Pulling this year's anthology together has been a rewarding experience for the Master of Publishing students and it is with some sadness (but mostly excitement) that the anthology has finally left our hands and rests in yours. None of this would have been possible without the invaluable input of some slightly more experienced in the art of publishing.

The editors would like to thank Fiona Giles and the Department of Media and Communications, and the School of Letters, Art and Media at the University of Sydney, Agata Mrva-Montoya and the Sydney University Press, PM Newton and of course Mark Rossiter for their contribution in guiding this anthology from a manuscript to a printed book.

The editors: Louisa Althans, Tori Brownrigg, Lex Hirst, Patrick Hsiao, Nadia Junaideen, Lindsay Liu, Pippa Lyons, Olivia Porter, Kristen Rooke, Lisa Schons, Kelly Stock and Veronica Tang.